Structured Deposition of Animal Remains in the Fertile Crescent during the Bronze Age

José Luis Ramos Soldado

Archaeopress Publishing Ltd
Gordon House
276 Banbury Road
Oxford OX2 7ED

www.archaeopress.com

ISBN 978 1 78491 272 7
ISBN 978 1 78491 269 7 (e-Pdf)

© Archaeopress and J L Ramos Soldado 2016

All rights reserved. No part of this book may be reproduced or transmitted,
in any form or by any means, electronic, mechanical, photocopying or otherwise,
without the prior written permission of the copyright owners.

Printed and bound in Great Britain by Marston Book Services Ltd, Oxfordshire

Contents

Abstract v
Acknowledgements vi
1. Introduction 1
2. Historical and archaeological context 3
3. Structured deposition of animal remains in the Fertile Crescent during the III Millennium BC 4
    3. 1. Structured deposition of animal remains in Syria during the III Millennium BC 4
        3. 1. 1. Tell Beydar 5
        3. 1. 2. Umm el-Marra 6
            Equids 6
            Dogs 8
            Pigs 8
            Bovids 8
        3. 1. 3. Tell Halawa 8
            Equids 8
            Ovicaprines 8
        3. 1. 4. Tell Banat 8
        3. 1. 5. Abu Hamad 9
        3. 1. 6. Tall Bi'a 9
        3. 1. 7. Nagar (Tell Brak) 10
            Equids 10
            Dogs 12
            Fish 13
    3. 2. Structured deposition of animal remains in Mesopotamia during the III Millennium BC ... 14
        3. 2. 1. al-'Usiyah 14
        3. 2. 2. Tell Madhhur 15
        3. 2. 3. Uch Tepe (Tell Razuk) 15
        3. 2. 4. Tell Abu Qasim 16
        3. 2. 5. Kish 16
        3. 2. 6. Abu Salabikh 17
            Equids 17
            Ovicaprines 18
        3. 2. 7. Nippur 20
            Equids 20
            Ovicaprines 21
        3. 2. 8. Lagash (Tell al-Hiba) 21
        3. 2. 9. Ur 21
        3. 2. 10. Additional information about other sites 25
4. Structured deposition of animal remains in the Fertile Crescent during the II Millennium BC 26
    4. 1. Structured deposition of animal remains in Mesopotamia during the II Millennium BC ... 26
        4. 1. 1. Tell Ababra 26
        4. 1. 2. Isin 26
    4. 2. Structured deposition of animal remains in Syria during the II Millennium BC 27
        4. 2. 1. Umm el-Marra 27
    4. 3. Structured deposition of animal remains in the Levant during the II Millennium BC 28
        4. 3. 1. Azor 28
        4. 3. 2. Sasa 29
        4. 3. 3. Tell 'Akko 29
        4. 3. 4. Megiddo 29
        4. 3. 5. Sidon 30
        4. 3. 6. Shechem 30
        4. 3. 7. Jericho 32

        Equids 32
        Ovicaprines 32
    4. 3. 8. Gezer 32
    4. 3. 9. Tell Beth-Shemesh 33
    4. 3. 10. Jebel Qa'aqir 33
    4. 3. 11. Tell el-'Ajjul 33
    4. 3. 12. Tell Jemmeh 33
    4. 3. 13. Tel Haror 33
    4. 3. 14. Additional information about other sites 34

5. Discussion 36

  5.1. Classification of the explained evidence 36
    Animal burials inside human graves 36
    Animal burials related to human graves 37
    Animal deposits unrelated to human graves 37
    Animals in sacred/ritual contexts 38
    Foundation deposits 38
    Animal remains in non-ritual contexts 38
  5. 2. Analysis and interpretation of taxa 38
    5. 2. 1. Equids 39
        Donkey 39
        Mule 41
        Onager 41
        Kúnga 41
    5. 2. 2. Dogs 42
    5. 2. 3. Sheeps and goats 45
    5. 2. 4. Bovids 46
    5. 2. 5. Pigs 46
    5. 2. 6. Birds 47
    5. 2. 7. Fish 48
  5. 3. Ritual and sacrifice in the frame of structured deposition of animal remains 48
  5. 4. Conclusions 50

6. Conclusions 52

Bibliography 53

Appendix A. Number of articulated animal individuals recorded at each site classified by species, region and period. 56

  Appendix A. A. Number of articulated animal individuals recorded at each site in Syria in the third millennium BC. 56
  Appendix A. B. Number of articulated animal individuals recorded at each site in Mesopotamia/Iraq in the third millennium BC. 56
  Appendix A. C. Number of articulated animal individuals recorded at each site in Mesopotamia/Iraq in the second millennium BC. 56
  Appendix A. D. Number of articulated animal individuals recorded at each site in the Levant in the second millennium BC. 57

Appendix B. Identification of equid species classified by site and period. 58

  Appendix B. A. Specie identification of equid individuals from sites dated to the third millennium BC. 58
  Appendinx B. B. Specie identification of equid individuals from sites dated to the second millennium BC. 58

List of Figures

Fig. 1. Map showing some of the sites discussed in section 3. 1. (Author). 4
Fig. 2. Illustration of demoiselle crane anthropoids virgo (after Van Neer, 2000). 5
Fig. 3. Articulated equid skeletons found in Installation G, Upper Layer (after Weber, 2012). 7
Fig. 4. Section of three main levels of occupation in the public sector at Tell Banat that includes the location of the foundation deposit behind Building 6 (after Porter, 2002b). 10
Fig. 5. Skeletons of donkeys 4 (up) and 5 (down) in the original situation they were found at the site (Clutton-Brock, 2001). 11
Fig. 6. The skeleton of the dog as it was found at Tell Brak (Clutton-Brock, 2001). 12
Fig. 7 Yellow-fin black porgy. 13
Fig. 8. The seabream skeleton from Tell Brak (Roselló Izquierdo & Morales Múñiz, 2001). 13
Fig. 9. Location of some of the sites discussed in this section (Author). 14
Fig. 10. Tell Madhhur tomb in Trench 5G (after Killick and Roaf, 1979). 15
Fig. 11. Burial 12 at Tell Razuk (after Zarins, 1986). 16
Fig. 12. A reconstruction of Burial II (after Zarins 1986). 17
Fig. 13. Articulated equid skeleton found in ash-tip at Abu Salabikh (after Postgate, 1986). 18
Fig. 14. Equids found at Grave 162 (after Postgate, 1986). 19
Fig. 15 Plan of Grave 162 showing the five equids in what have been considered their original position (after Postgate, 1983). 19
Fig. 16. Plan of Burial 14, Level XIIIB Chamber (after McMahon, 2006). 20
Fig. 17. Equid skeleton at Burial 14 (after McMahon, 2006). 21
Fig. 18. Ovicaprine skeletons located next to skeleton 3 at Burial 14 (after McMahon, 2006). 22
Fig. 19. Articulated onager skeleton found at Lagash (Area C) (after Zarins 1986). 22
Fig. 20. Plan of PG 789 (after Baadsgaard et al., 2012). 23
Fig. 21. Plan of PG 800 (after Baadsgaard et al., 2012). 24
Fig. 22. Some of the sites discussed in this section (Author). 28
Fig. 23. Bovid skeleton found in Tomb 903 at Megiddo (after Guy, 1938). 29
Fig. 24. Sheep skeleton in Burial 99, Sidon (after Doument-Serhal, 2013). 30
Fig. 25. Ovicaprine skeleton found at Shechem in locus 6:18 in Room 8 (after Campbell, 2002). ...31
Fig. 26. Equid skeleton found at Shechem (after Campbell, 2002). 31
Fig. 27. Equid skeleton found at Locus 10066 (after Leger & Zeder, 1988). 32
Fig. 28. Raven skeleton found at loculi 8430/82091 at Tel Haror, associated with the mandible of a lamb (after Klenck, 2002). 34
Fig. 29. Articulated puppy skeleton found in loculi 8430/82443 at Tel Haror (after Klenck, 2002)..35
Fig. 30. Articulated skeleton of a juveline dog associated with the fragmented remains of a raven at Tel Haror (after Klenck, 2002). 35
Fig. 31. Some kúnga pulling from battle wagons depicted in the Standard of Ur (2600 BC) (after Littauer & Crouwel, 1979). 41

List of Tables

Table 1. Chronology of the Bronze Age for the Ancient Near East. 3
Table 2. Chronology of the Bronze Age for Mesopotamia (after Cryer, 1995)....................3
Table. 3. Age, sex, position and orientation of the donkey skeletons found at Tell Brak (after Clutton-Brock, 2001). 12
Table. 4. Age ratio of animals found in Shaft 1 (after Schwartz, 2013)............................27

Abstract

Although most of the animal remains recorded throughout the archaeological excavations consist usually of large assemblages of discarded and fragmented bones, it is possible to yield articulated animal skeletons in some cases. Most of them have been usually picked up from sacred and/or funerary contexts, but not all of them might fit necessarily in ritual and symbolic interpretations, and not all of the structured deposit of animal remains may be explained due to anthropic factors. In addition, zooarchaeology has traditionally focused on animal domestication, husbandry and economy, and species identification above all, shutting out further discussion about these type of findings. Moreover, the limited condition of the data is also another issue to bear in mind. Thus, the aim of this paper has been to draw up a literature review of the structured deposits of animal remains during the third and second millennia BC in the Ancient Near East for its subsequent classification and detailed interpretation. In this survey it has been attested that not only most of the articulated animal remains have been found in ritual and/or funerary contexts but also that all species recorded– but some exceptions–are domestic. Hence, I argue in this paper that there is a broad religious attitude towards the main domesticated animals of human economy in the An-cient Near East, based on the closeness of these animals to the human sphere. Therefore, it seems that domesticated animals were powerful constituents in the cultural landscape of these regions, never simply resources.

This paper is the result of the author's own work. Material from the published and unpublished work of others, which is referred to in the paper, is credited to the author(s) in question in the text.

Acknowledgements

I would not have been able to draw up this essay without the support of several persons who have given me their help and dedication with total patience. First of all, I would like to show my most honest gratitude to Dr. Penny Wilson, who has been a mentor for me since the first minute I arrived in Durham, and to Dr. Derek Kennet, since without his attention and willingness perhaps I would have never decided to come. Secondly, I need to display my everlasting thanks to two good friends of mine whose help has been crucial: María Martín Mayorga, restorer, who has helped me retouching and improving all the pictures included in this paper; as well as María Martínez Velázquez, lawyer, and Elisa Ramos Romero, English philologist, who have supervised the text, something actually important due to my struggle with the English language in this, my first year abroad. And last but definitely not least, I really want to thank those people who made this dream possible: Dr. Marta Díaz-Zorita Bonilla, archaeologist (University of Tübingen), who has been always there in every moment since I took the decision of studying at Durham and whose support and patience have been eternal. That is also the case of Dr. Graham Philip, my supervisor, who has been always there providing me all the feedback I need as well as his guidance and support even when my bad organisation made me not worth of it. Finally, I dedicate this dissertation to my parents, whose backing and love made possible for me to be writing these words right now.

To all of them, thanks.

1. Introduction

The study of archaeofanual remains has mainly contributed to unravelling the origin of food production termed in the 'Neolithic Revolution', as well as to chronology and domestication, tracing the origin and evolution of livestock breeds (Davis, 1987: 20-21). In general, zooarchaeology is a resourceful and key discipline in reconstructing the environment of the past human societies.

Most of the animal remains recorded throughout the archaeological excavations consist usually of large assemblages of discarded and fragmented bones yielded from middens and domestic contexts. However, sometimes it is possible to find complete articulated individuals that appear usually in sacred and/or funerary contexts. Reasons behind such findings may be numerous, and their good state of preservation may not necessarily imply anthropic factors. Nevertheless, this kind of findings is rare and noteworthy, not always easy to interpret and understand. Thus, the aim of my dissertation is to develop single and coherent framework for the analysis and research of structured deposits of animal remains in non-domestic wastes and contexts in the Fertile Crescent–with the exception of Egypt, due to the limited nature of this paper–during the Bronze Age, in order to understand the meaning and socio-ideological significance of this phenomenon.

Among the key aims of this paper lie to develop a classification of the different types of structured deposits of animal bone remains depending on their contexts and further interpretation, in order to classify the evidence for a comparative evaluation as efficient as possible. In addition, I prepare to figure out any possible belief and cultic practice–if any–behind each type of deposit and their relation to each animal species, as well as to evaluate how and in which level the socio-economic and ideological changes of these cultures within the Bronze Age may affect this phenomenon. Unlike what it may seem, for such objectives a deep literature review is needed.

Although the study of topics such as animal offerings and burial, associated in most of cases with this kind of deposits, may generally be of little interest within the academic field due to an apparent strong database, what is certain is that this subject needs a deep literature review. This is not only due to the insufficient documentation published by previous generations of archaeologist. The bibliography is overall inconsistent, as well as the archaeological record. There are some reports where the information concerning faunal remains is deeply detailed, including references even to the sex, age, position and orientation of the articulated animal individuals, distinguished from the discarded ones. However, the majority of the reports does not include such detailed information and provide only basic data about the faunal assemblages. This unequal quality within the evidence would be unavoidably perceived all over this essay since there are plenty of information about some sites while barely a couple of lines about other ones. In addition, there are sites whose reports have not been updated or where new research has not been carried out, and I was even unable to access to some of them.

The limited nature of the evidence is also related to the fact that zooarchaeological research is usually focused on economy and husbandry, specie identification and animal domestication, shutting out other topics. Indeed, few zooarchaeological publications have focused on ritual and religion. Four main reasons for this have been pointed out (O'Day et al., 2004: xiii): first, sacred sites are usually inaccessible to archaeologists; second, some zooarchaeologists have traditionally claimed that ideological issues are either unimportant or are not subjects that this kind of studies can reliably contribute to; third, zooarchaeology tends to operate autonomously from other areas of both archaeology and anthropology; and four, faunal remains are rarely collected and/or analysed, as I have previously stated. Moreover, most of the reports that include a more detailed research about such topics are usually focused on offering and sacrifice, and with the exception of donkey burial, most of the information of this kind of topics is provided by the written sources rather than through the archaeological record. Woefully, textual evidence is also limited. Due to this hard scenario I needed to complete the information from the archaeological record with the information recorded at the texts.

Moreover, issues do not lie only in the quality of the bibliography. The understanding of the taphonomic processes is a key for the interpretation of findings of these types, and they are not always easy to interpret. There are discarded and fragmented bone remains that could constitute whole articulated skeletons back in time but that have been disturbed in time for several reasons. In the same way, deliberated burials can include disarticulated as well as articulated skeletal remains. Hence, the context is often more important than the finding itself, and the structured deposition of animal remains may not be interpreted as a phenomenon by itself at first sight. For such reasons I will include or allude remains from some sites that have not been found necessarily articulated but fit the type of evidence that I aim to compile in this survey.

This dissertation is structured in several sections which cover different aspects of this research. After a brief description of the historical and archaeological context of the Bronze Age–a necessary step in every historical research–the compiled data are organised by time and space for the consideration of their features and contexts in order to develop a solid comparative evaluation. Despite a detailed discussion section is worked out in the second half of the dissertation, main details and interpretations are provided in the sections of each site, in order to acquaint the reader with the evidence by establishing the bases of the further discussion of the framework exposed on this paper. I consider this structure the most suitable for this kind of essay according to the reports of similar research that I have consulted.

2. Historical and archaeological context

According to both archaeological evidence and cuneiform archives such as those from the *Palace G* from Ebla, in the late third millennium BC took place what it is called "the second urban revolution". During this phenomenon states, cities, monumental architecture and intensified economic specialisation appeared in Syria and upper Mesopotamia (Schwartz, 2013: 497-498). However, urban disintegration appears by the later centuries, thus taking place a decentralisation process. Following this period of instability, new polities emerged in the early second millennium B. C, identified with the Amorites (Schwartz, 2013: 498).

On the subject of chronology, problems in attempting to establish a uniform chronology for the Ancient Near East have always arisen. Due to all the issues which entail this task, it is recently more frequent to refer to the millennium at issue instead of using named periods. There are several different tables of chronology, each one applicable to a different region. From these I will use the most basic one concerning the Bronze Age, overall applicable to all the regions (table 1), which is the most common chronology table I found within the reports. However, I will also include a detailed chronology – if provided – of each site.

	EBA I	3300-3000 BC
Early Bronze Age	EBA II	3000-2700 BC
(EBA: 3300-2100 BC)	EBA III	2700-2200 BC
	EBA IV	2200-2100 BC
	MBA I	2100-2000 BC
Middle Bronze Age	MBA II A	2000-1750 BC
(MBA: 2100-1550 BC)	MBA IIB	1750-1650 BC
	MBA IIC	1650-1550 BC
Late Bronze Age	LBA I	1550-1400 BC
(LBA: 1550-1200 BC)	LBA IIA	1400-1300 BC
	LBA IIB	1300-1200 BC

TABLE 1. CHRONOLOGY OF THE BRONZE AGE FOR THE ANCIENT NEAR EAST.

In the case of Mesopotamia, whatever the reason, this table is less often used. Hence, I decided to also include in this section a reference table for the chronology of Mesopotamia (table 2), which is used in the reports in most cases.

Early Dynastic I	2900-2700 BC	EBA II
Early Dynastic II	2700-2600 BC	EBA III
Early Dynastic III	2600-2350 BC	EBA III
Empire of Akkad	2350-2193 BC	EBA III-IV
Old Babylonian period	2000-1600 BC	MBA IIB-C

TABLE 2. CHRONOLOGY OF THE BRONZE AGE FOR MESOPOTAMIA (AFTER CRYER, 1995).

3. Structured deposition of animal remains in the Fertile Crescent during the III Millennium BC

In this section I will present the articulated skeletal remains from the archaeological record yielded from Mesopotamia and Syria since no deposits of this kind are attested in the Levant. Sites are explained from north to south according to their geographical location.

3. 1. Structured deposition of animal remains in Syria during the III Millennium BC

'Chariot burials' feature the structured deposits of animal remains in Syria during the third millennium BC, as it happens in Mesopotamia. As it can be observed, most of the equids found in human funerary contexts in Syria during the third millennium BC were donkeys, but some exceptions include *kúnga*, a highly valued donkey-onager hybrid.

Although the equid bone samples are sparse and not very important, their relative high frequency reactivates the debate about their role in Early Bronze Age societies in Syria, as it has been pointed out (Vila, 2006: 101). On the other hand, it has been argued that ovicaprine deposits in graves in the third millennium BC at Syria generally bear characteristics of food offerings since they usually occur in selected quarters (Vila, 2006: 116-117).

Unlike in Mesopotamia, where complex hierarchical systems are already consolidated, in Syria during the third millennium is taking place a complex transition from communal socio-political structures based on kinship to social structures more polarised where an elite that outstands from the rest of the population is gradually monopolising the power. In this context, religion and ritual are used to manipulate memory in order to legitimate the possession of power by the elites. Since

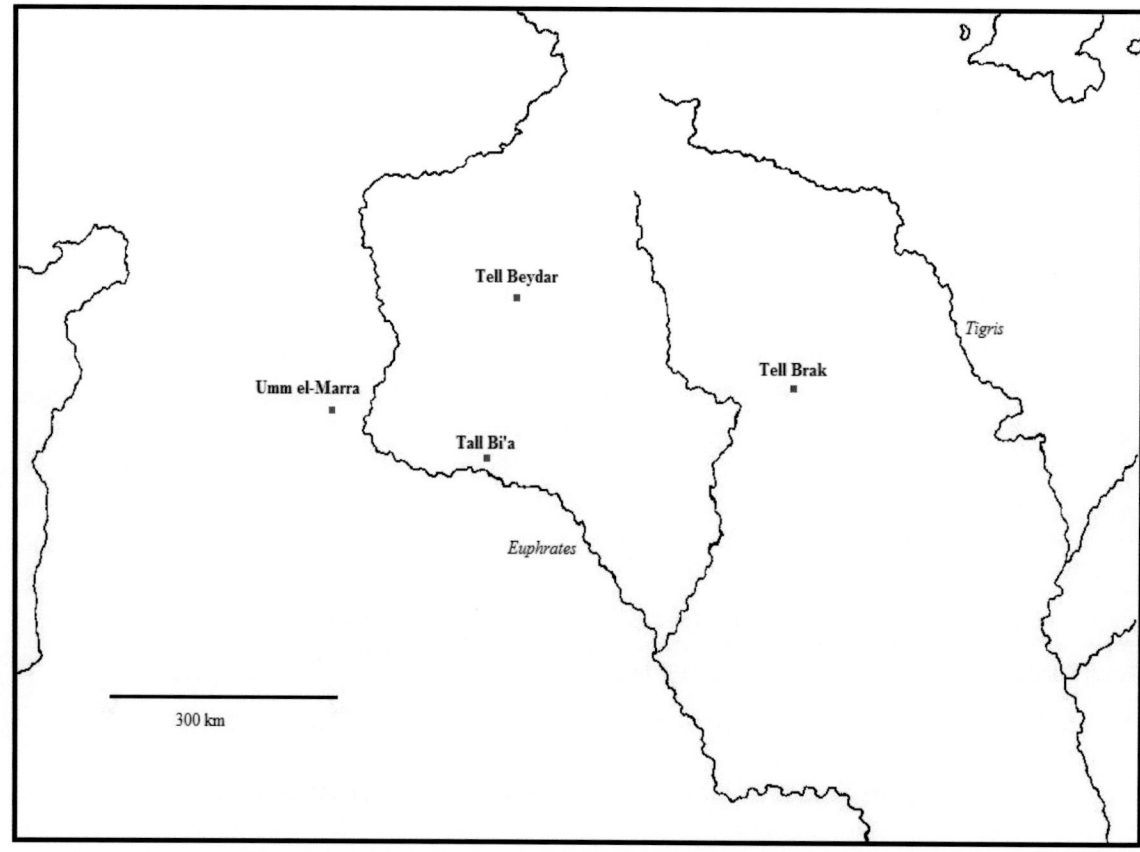

FIG. 1. MAP SHOWING SOME OF THE SITES DISCUSSED IN SECTION 3. 1. (AUTHOR).

structured animal deposits usually appear associated with ritual and funerary contexts in this period, they are closely related to this complex socio-political transition, where enigmatic ceremonies of difficult interpretation occur. Indeed, written sources give us information about how in Mari and Ebla most people maintained an identity by both "tribe" and "town", and how "ancestors" operated in the legitimation of an exclusionary system (Porter, 2002a: 171; 2002b: 28-29). It is likely to think that this situation is reflected in sites such as Umm el-Marra or Tell Banat, where complex socio-political transformation towards more hierarchical systems in the frame of the urban revolution is happening.

3. 1. 1. Tell Beydar

Two complete birds skeletons assigned to demoiselle cranes (*demoiselle crane anthropoides virgo*) (fig. 2) were found associated with a human skeleton in a grave dated to the Old Akkadian period at Tell Beydar, ancient Nabada (northern Syria) (Van Neer, 2000: 61). The sex of both individuals has not been able to be identified. Concerning this strange finding, with parallel in Nagar, is difficult to interpret. It has been argued that the yearly arrival and departure of the flocks of this specie probably were well-known in the region and due to the predictability of this phenomenon the population may have given a special meaning to these birds (Van Neer, 2000: 62).

FIG. 2. ILLUSTRATION OF *DEMOISELLE CRANE ANTHROPOIDS VIRGO* (AFTER VAN NEER, 2000).

Several other animals of the same spectrum of species found in Syria (including vultures as in Umm el-Marra) dating from the third millennium BC have been found at this site, although discarded. Nevertheless, I consider this fact worth of mention since some of the bones assemblages might be whole individuals at the time they were deposited (Van Neer & De Cupere, 2000: 69-79). In addition, complete dog and equid individuals have been found in Hellenistic times.

3. 1. 2. Umm el-Marra

Umm el-Marra is an early urban centre of 20-25 hectares located in the Jabbul plain of western Syria between Aleppo and the Euphrates valley. Topographically, it is a fortified low mound with an acropolis in the south centre. This site is smaller than the major urban centers of Syria such as Ebla, Mari or Aleppo, which has led to consider it as a regional centre subservient of those larger ones, due also to its situation on the communication route between the Euphrates river and these powerful cities (Weber, 2012: 162-164; Schwartz, 2013: 495-497).

Umm el-Marra was founded in the early third millennium BC but it was mainly occupied along the third and second millennia, when large-scale societal complexity emerged in Syria as well as its early episodes of centralisation and decentralization took place (Schwartz, 2013: 496-498). By 2500-2200 BC the centre of the acropolis of this site was used as an elite mortuary complex, where several articulated animal skeletons have been found (Schwartz, 2013: 495, 498). Young ovicaprines and birds (such as ducks and geese) were buried whole while adult ovicaprines and bovids were butchered before being deposited in the tombs, where large numbers of vessels for food and drink have been also found (Weber, 2012: 164). All of these findings may suggest feasting rituals and ceremonies linked to the burials. Other cultic activities might be related to the delivered deposition of whole young animal individuals apart from equids and dogs, but there is no further information in the bibliography concerning them, so it is not possible neither to assess their meaning nor understanding the rituals they belonged to.

The central location and visibility of the tombs imply that this complex dominated the community and it was where ceremonies of ancestor veneration took place. Considering all of this, the dead here interred (both humans and animals) should have a high and special status and they continued playing an active role in the life of the community in spite of being in the afterlife. In such scenario, this elite funerary complex provided a constant reminder of the everlasting social hierarchy of the community and how things should work (Schwartz, 2013: 505-506). It has been argued that animals also played an important role in this funerary landscape, having a quasi human-like status. Nevertheless, equid tombs were subterranean while human tombs were above ground and larger, which means that their significance and ideological value was logically higher (Schwartz, 2013: 506).

Equids

Around 40 equid skeletons appeared at Umm el-Marra, 25 of them being complete (Weber, 2012: 165). They have been found not only associated with human burials but also in separate interments in the centre of the complex. All of them were males, and identified as *kunga*, some of them arranged symmetrically within the graves as a team to pull a vehicle, displaying also pathologies that suggest these animals were used as burden and loading beasts (Weber, 2012: 165; Schwartz, 2013: 498-499). The presence of these animals had a dual intention: on the one hand, it was aimed to display the social position and wealth of the humans related to them; on the other hand, they had to serve as transportation for the dead in the afterlife. It has been found out that both the young individuals and the aged ones were healthy and cared for well, but the younger equids were killed whilst the aged ones died naturally. Concerning this issue, it has been argued that the younger ones were killed ritually as a sacrifice to serve the dead, and the old ones were included in the grave as "treasures" in order to be used in the afterlife (Weber, 2012: 165; Schwartz, 2013: 499).

Since this mortuary complex changed through time, new tombs were added to the old ones. In the same way, equid installations were placed near earlier installations or above them (Schwartz, 2013: 499). According to patterns of architecture and the age of the equids, four types of equids installations have been identified at Umm el-Marra (Weber, 2012: 165-168; Schwartz, 2013: 499):

- Type I: subterranean mudbrick or stone structures that contained young equid individuals on standing position, some of them disturbed after the collapse of the roof and some walls of these structures. Human infants appeared also in these structures, but they were deposited after such disturbances, so there was no link between the equids and them.
- Type II: mudbrick structures of two compartments with a standing aged equid individual facing west in each of them. This type of installations also contained additional deposits of discarded bones of other animals (such as other equids and dogs), pottery vessels and even human infant remains. We should ask ourselves if the equids were the ones deposited to be related to the human infants or if it was the opposite situation. Did the equids have a higher ideological significance than human babies at Umm el-Marra? If so, why? Woefully, there is not enough information to achieve any consensus without developing a speculative rather than an empirical discussion.
- Type III: only a single structure, a pit containing four delivered deposited and articulated equids of young age, in addition with several disarticulated equid individuals in higher layers (fig. 3).
- Type IV: outside structures associated with Tomb 8 that contained individual equid skeletons.

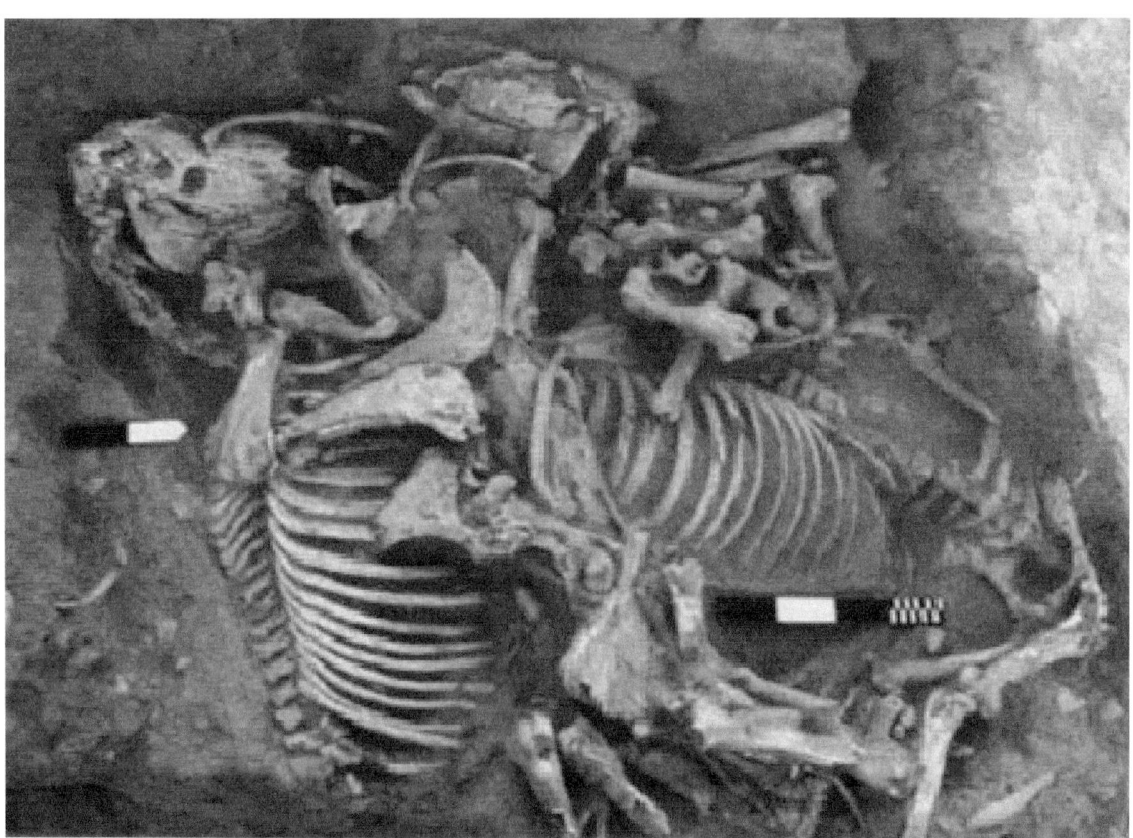

Fig. 3. Articulated equid skeletons found in Installation G, Upper Layer (after Weber, 2012).

Dogs

In the northwest of *Tomb 6*, the earliest and the largest one, there was a burned room that contained three puppy skeletons, one located in the southwest corner, another located in the northeast one, and the last one located in the southeast corner. Furthermore, in the space between this tomb and *Installation E* another puppy skeleton and two puppy skulls were found. The burning of these spaces with these animals *in situ* and their probable link to equid installations of Type I may imply ritual connotations for these interments, as it has been indicated (Schwartz, 2013: 500-501). However, there is no further information concerning the two puppy skulls and their situation or context, it is not possible to know if they are part of what once were two articulated skeletons that did not preserve well or aversely the skulls were placed separately.

Other six puppy skeletons were found in *Installation B* of *Tomb 1*, related to equid installations of Type II, three of them in each of its two chambers (Schwartz, 2013: 503-504). Thus, there are a total of ten articulated puppy skeletons associated with the graves of Umm el-Marra.

Pigs

A single piglet skeleton was found in the southeast corner of the room next to *Tomb 6* with the rest of the puppies, and in particular next to one of them (Schwartz, 2013: 501).

Bovids

In a "U"-shaped room at the northwest of *Tomb 5* it was found a bovid skeleton associated with the remains of two line jugs. According to the excavations reports, activities within these rooms are likely to have been related to the rituals and ceremonies attending the corpses interred in the tombs (Schwartz, 2013: 502), which lead us to think about this bovid individual as a ritual sacrifice, although there is no further information in the bibliography about it.

3. 1. 3. Tell Halawa

Tell Halawa is located in Northern Syria on the Euphrates River. Several articulated animal remains related to human graves have been found at this place, dating from 2200-2100 BC (Zarins, 1986: 175-176; Philip, 1995: 151; Way, 2011: 136).

Equids

Three adult donkeys, two females and one male, appeared inside the tomb of a human man (*Grave H-70*) who was also accompanied by two daggers and even a human girl, clearly associated with him (Zarins, 1986: 175-176; Philip, 1995: 151; Way, 2011: 136). This find may be interpreted as a warrior burial due to the funerary furnishing that appears related to the male and the features of the burial in general.

Ovicaprines

Two complete sheep skeletons, one of them from an adult and the other one from a sub-adult, were found in a grave at this site (Vila, 2006: 116-117).

3. 1. 4. Tell Banat

The Tell Banat settlement complex is located on the east bank of the Euphrates River, approximately 50 km of the Turkish border. It consists of a group of sites of varying sizes and functions dating from 2600 to 2450 BC, whose main central urban settlement was Tell Banat itself. Since some palaces and public buildings have been identified in this site, it is argued that it held the authority structures of a state (Porter, 2002a: 158). Animal remains at this site have been found in the so-called White Monument A and in Public Building B6.

The "White Monuments" at Tell Banat consist of a series of mortuary structures comprised in a tall conical mound located at the north of the site, dated from 2700 to 2300 BC. White Monument A, the last version of this mortuary mound (dating from 2450-2300 BC) contained several discrete burial deposits that were interred as the mound was compiled. All humans remains that appeared in this structure were disarticulated and mixed or related to animal bones and ceramics (Porter, 2002a: 160-164; 2002b: 16; Way, 2011: 136). According to the reports, 40% of animal bones are from equid, with a secondary concentration of bovid bones. In contrast, the below group of tombs have no equid, few cattle and a high proportion of ovicaprines. Finally, 80% of animal bones from the whole site consist of ovicaprines (Porter, 2002a: 165; 2002b: 21; Way, 2011: 136-137). Despite these animal remains are fragmentary and disarticulated, I included them in this paper since they are secondary burial deposits and therefore they were once structured animal deposits.

Although the fragmentary condition of the bones does not allow us to elaborate a clear interpretation, the inclusion of equid bones only in White Monument A may be an indicator of a high socio-economic status and therefore of a differential social position of the dead–which is anyway attested by other factors–displaying a seeking of legitimation from this people within the traditional social structure, i. e. the kin-based communal system, in order to obtain a defined distinction from the rest of the social group and the community in general (Porter, 2002a: 170-171; 2002b: 21-24). It has been also argued that equid were included within the graves as funerary furnishings in order to be useful for the afterlife (Way, 2011: 137). Woefully, none of these interpretations can be solidly stated without further osteological analyses providing information about the possible pathologies of the equids (if any) as well as the cause of their death.

As it has been also pointed out, some parallelisms can be stated between this site and Umm el-Marra. On the one hand, some individuals have been identified with onager, other ones with half-ass (possibly *kúnga*), which may lead us to think that this elite probably possessed *kúnga,* as well all the elite from Umm el-Marra, from where they probably obtained their own ones. In this case, equid remains would constitute a clear marker of prestige. On the other hand, it has been claimed that equid remains may represent ritual sacrifices dedicated to the dead as it happened at Umm el-Marra (Way, 2011: 137). We have to bear in mind that these possibilities may not be exclusive and can occur simultaneously, thus equid were sacrificed as part of the funerary ceremonies that took place, and later included as grave goods and also elite markers.

The second animal deposit from this site worth mentioning in this survey is the one found beneath *Building 6*. Fragmentary equid remains appeared under this building related to some pottery vessels (fig. 4), which may lead us to interpret this finding as a foundation deposit (Way, 2011: 137).

3. 1. 5. Abu Hamad

Abu Hamad is located in the foothills of the Jebel Bishri, close to the Euphrates Valley. Three domestic donkey skeletons were found in a cist tomb (A5) in the necropolis of this site, two adults and one sub-adult, all of them in anatomic connection despite their bad state of preservation, and dating from the Early Bronze Age IV (2200-2100 BC) (Vila, 2006: 116). Woefully, there is not further information about their position neither orientation nor pathologies in the reports.

3. 1. 6. Tall Bi'a

Tall Bi'a is located at the confluence of the Balikh and the Euphrates Rivers (Way, 2011: 137). The earliest attested to be buried donkey in Syria was found at this site, dating to ca. 2500 BC, almost contemporary to the individual recorded at Tarkhan, in Egypt (Vila, 2006: 115, 117). This finding consists of an intact donkey burial in a small shaft located under a human tomb (*Burial U:22*) (Way, 2011: 137).

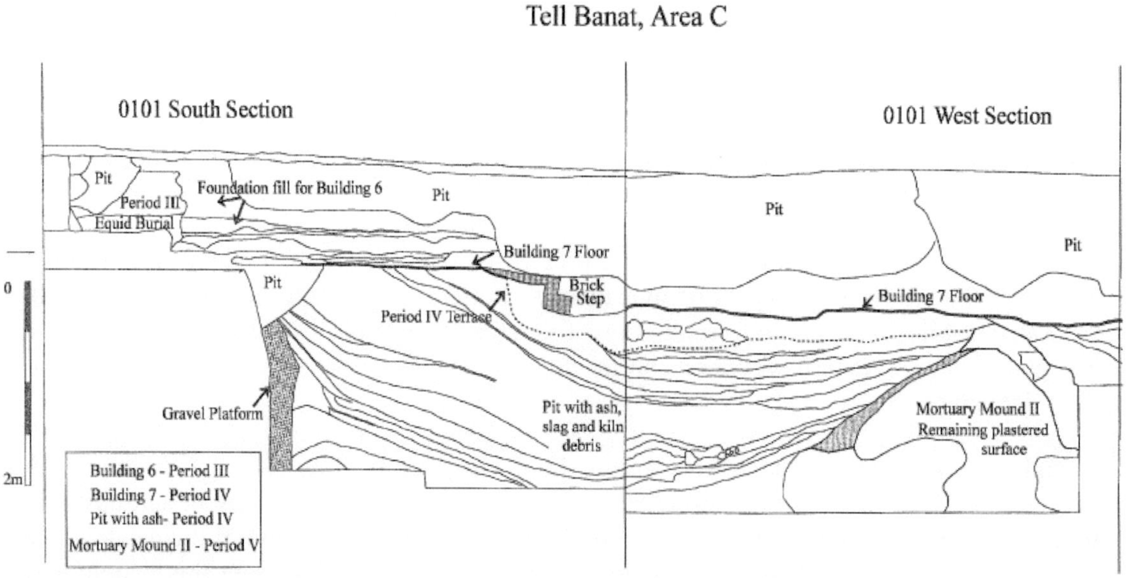

FIG. 4. SECTION OF THREE MAIN LEVELS OF OCCUPATION IN THE PUBLIC SECTOR AT TELL BANAT THAT INCLUDES THE LOCATION OF THE FOUNDATION DEPOSIT BEHIND BUILDING 6 (AFTER PORTER, 2002B).

3. 1. 7. Nagar (Tell Brak)

The city of Nagar dominated the plains of north-eastern Syria in the third millennium BC. We know through the cuneiform texts of Ebla that this urban centre had the same status than other great centers such as Mari and Kish, and it was a major focus of contact between Nineveh and the Tigris Valley (Oates et al., 2008: 390).

Equids

Six complete domestic donkey skeletons appeared ritually deposited in a large public monumental building in this site, dating around 2550 BC through radiocarbon analyses (Clutton-Brock, 2001: 327, 336; Vila, 2006: 116). This building was related to a temple dedicated to Samagan, god of the animals of the steppe. We know through cuneiform documents that this place was related to the breeding and trading of *kúnga* equids. Sometime around 2300 BC, this complex was temporarily abandoned and later deliberately emptied and infilled. Valuable offerings have been deposited on the top of this fill, including also other donkey skeletons remains (Oates et al., 2008: 391). The careful deposition of these equids and the other ritual deposits around them may suggest they were deliberately deposited and probably with ritual connotations. After all, donkey was a symbol of fertility in Ancient Near East and it was sacrificed as part of treats and ceremonies (Clutton-Brock, 2001: 331).

One of them (donkey 6) was identified as a *kúnga* (Vila, 2006: 116; Oates *et al.*, 2008: 391). It was found near to the skeleton of a dog, having both of them been buried at the same time. There is no evidence about the deaths of both animals or if their deaths were connected. This donkey individual was probably covered with soil and, as well as the dog, was buried very quickly before decomposition occurred, which explains the moulded form of both animals and the survival of many of their tiny bones (Clutton-Brock, 2001: 329-331).

Due to the state of preservation of these equids, there is no evidence about how they were killed or how they died, although it is likely to think that most of them probably were probably killed *in situ* according to their position. Donkeys 1, 2 and 3 were interred together in one of the rooms of the building (called *Room 10*). Donkeys 1 and 2 were lying as a pair, with donkey 3 lying behind them facing the opposite direction. The fourth donkey was buried in the east courtyard doorway of another room of the building (*Room 2*), while the fifth one was lying in the courtyard itself (fig. 2). All of them were lying with the limbs faced downwards the body but donkey 4 due to lack of space at first sight (Clutton-Brock, 2001: 334-336). It seems there is not a pattern of positioning neither orientation of the equid skeletons at Tell Brak, at least according to the age and sex of these individuals (fig. 3).

Fig. 5. Skeletons of donkeys 4 (up) and 5 (down) in the original situation they were found at the site (Clutton-Brock, 2001).

	Age	Sex	Lying side	Orientation
Donkey 1	Aged adult	Female	Left	Southeast
Donkey 2	Young adult	Female	Left	Southwest
Donkey 3	Young adult	Male	Left	North
Donkey 4	Aged adult	Male	Right	North
Donkey 5	Aged adult	Female	Left	East
Donkey 6	Adult	Female	Left	-

TABLE. 3. AGE, SEX, POSITION AND ORIENTATION OF THE DONKEY SKELETONS FOUND AT TELL BRAK (AFTER CLUTTON-BROCK, 2001).

No serious pathologies were attested on any of the skeletons, so in this case we are dealing with healthy individuals. The only issue, according to osteoarchaeological and zoological analyses, is that these donkeys were used as riding and/or pack animals. It can be proved that the six animals were well cared for, housed in stalls but being used with frequency as pack animals or ridden or harnessed to chariots (which have been recorded from contemporary levels at the site). It has been pointed out that all of them were sacrificed at the same time in order to satisfy thoroughly a demanding god (Clutton-Brock, 2001: 336-338).

Fragmented remains of animal bones from domestic pig, cattle, ovicaprines and even other equids were found associated with the skeletons of these donkeys. In this case, these bones were butchered and burned (Clutton-Brock, 2001: 329; Weber, 2001: 345). These issues, in my opinion, are surely an indication of feasting and consumption, probably part of the ceremonies that accompanied the rituals that involved the sacrifices of these animals. Moreover, most of the equids remains of these bones fragments in non ritual deposits have been identified as onager, which can lead us to think that they held a lower ideological significance compared to the donkey.

Dogs

A complete dog skeleton was discovered within the monumental building associated with the temple to the god Samagan where the donkey skeletons were found (fig. 6). Researchers suggest that this

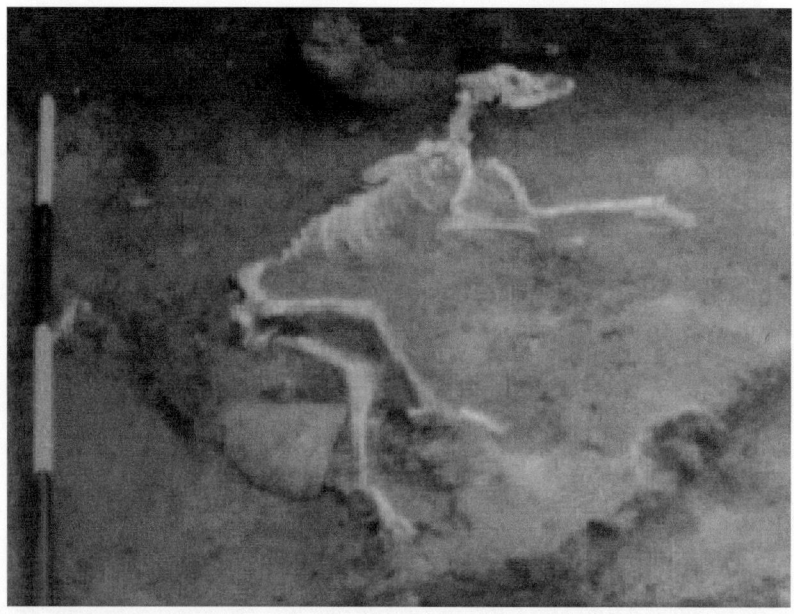

FIG. 6. THE SKELETON OF THE DOG AS IT WAS FOUND AT TELL BRAK (CLUTTON-BROCK, 2001).

dog was ritually buried at the time this building was filled in, as well as one of the donkeys (donkey 6), not long after 2250 BC. It is an adult male that was found on its left side in a like-running position, and it has been identified as a greyhound (Clutton-Brock, 2001: 327-328).

We know that greyhounds are one of the oldest dog breeds in the world, used for hunting in ancient times. It is widely depicted in pictorial representations from the second millennium BC in Egypt, for example (Clutton-Brock, 2001: 328-329).

Fish

The articulated skeleton of a yellow-fin black porgy (*acanthopagrus latus*) (fig. 7), dating on the early XXII century BC after the collapse of the Akkadian authority, was found in an ordinary household debris in the site of Tell Brak (fig. 8) (Roselló Izquierdo & Morales Múñiz, 2001: 339). This fish species is common along the shores of the Persian Gulf, and it has been yielded in several sites from the third millennium in Mesopotamia, but never previously in Syria. Furthermore, those finds have been found only in graves, so it is likely to consider symbolical and/or ritual significance for this species in Mesopotamia (Roselló Izquierdo & Morales Múñiz, 2001: 339-343).

FIG. 7 YELLOW-FIN BLACK PORGY.

FIG. 8. THE SEABREAM SKELETON FROM TELL BRAK (ROSELLÓ IZQUIERDO & MORALES MÚÑIZ, 2001).

3. 2. Structured deposition of animal remains in Mesopotamia during the III Millennium BC

Most of the structured depositions of animal remains in Mesopotamia during the III Millennium BC consist of (an) equid(s) deliberately deposited in human graves, exhibited in pairs and related to draft implements in most sites (Way, 2011: 141). Donkey burials and "chariot burials" are well known in Mesopotamia, and the texts provide information about the high-status of equids as well as the ethnographic research (Zarins, 1986: 164). However, little is known about the practice of animal burial in Mesopotamia not only in earlier periods but also in later ones, and known cuneiform texts are totally silent about this phenomenon (Zarins, 1986: 164, 168).

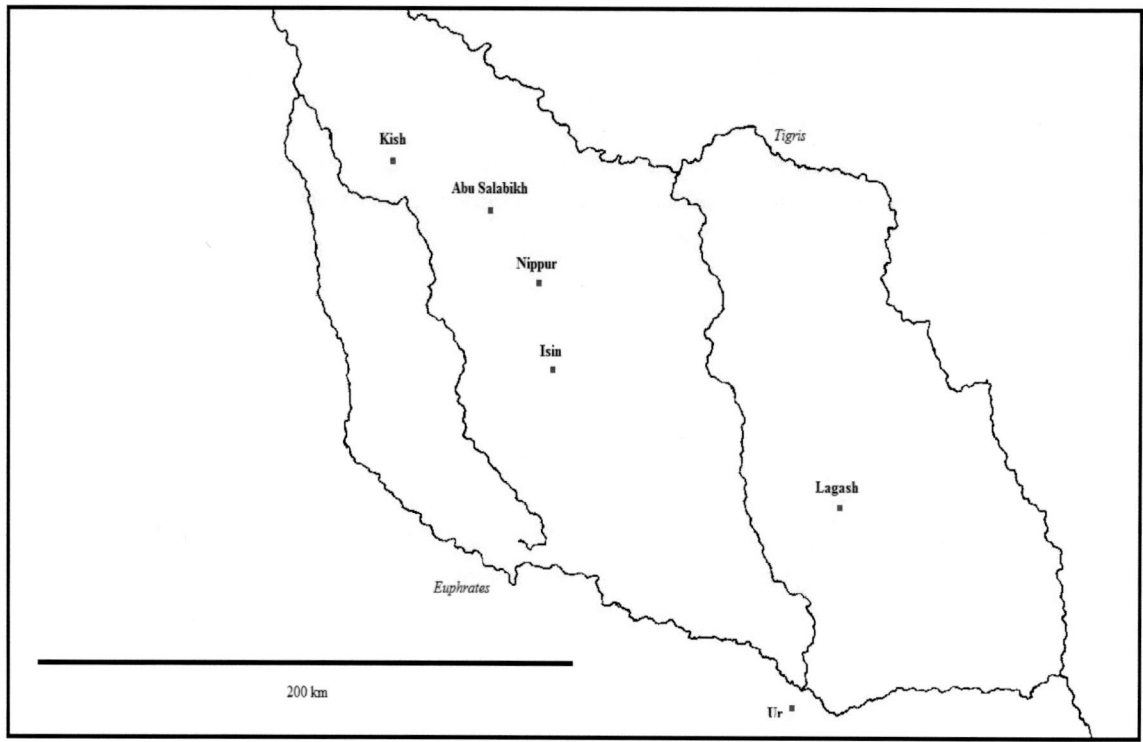

Fig. 9. Location of some of the sites discussed in this section (Author).

Most of the equids have been identified as donkeys, but there are also several onager and even hybrid individuals. Although the animals interred in human graves have been generally interpreted as funerary goods, this issue is subject of discussion, and funerary contexts are not the only ones were articulated skeletons of animal have been found, as we will see.

Animal interments are usually associated to the phenomenon of the 'warrior burials' in this region and period. As it happens concerning this type of burials, structured deposits of animal remains present both regional and temporal variations, but their resemblances suggest a unity of underlying structure that continue in later periods.

3. 2. 1. al-'Usiyah

In this site, located in the Haditha basin of the Euphrates River, a stone-built chamber tomb probably dated to ED III (ca. 2600-2300 BC) was discovered. Although this tomb was disturbed in antiquity, it was possible to record the presence of four equids in poor state of preservation placed outside the front of the tomb and related to a copper ring. Woefully, no further analyses have been carried out to date and there is no more information about them (Zarins, 1986: 175; Way, 2011: 142).

3. 2. 2. Tell Madhhur

Tell Madhuur is located on the northeast area of the Himrin basin to be flooded when the dam is completed. It is a low mound whose most of its deposits date from Late Ubaid and Early Dynastic I periods, although this site was also used for occasional elite burials in Akkadian times (Killick & Roaf, 1979: 541-542). Several articulated animal remains have been found at this site in three different graves of ED I town levels (ca. 2800 BC). A complex tomb structure in disturbed state placed at *Trench 7D/E* and dated to ED II-III harboured two unidentified equid skeletons related to a missing human body that was also surrounded by ceramic vessels. Another tomb was discovered in *Trench 5G*, dating around 2300-2200 BC. It contained the body of an adult man associated with two donkey skeletons (fig. 10), one of them in prone position and the other one lying on its left side, both placed side by side as if yoked together. Other grave goods such as metal items, food offering remains and ceramic vessels were also related to the human body. A puppy skeleton was also found between the equids, but there is no further information about it in the bibliography (Killick & Roaf, 1979: 540; Zarins, 1986: 172-174; Philip, 1995: 149; Way, 2011: 142-143).

The presence of bronze items identified as string notches and goads and the position of the equids as teaming up have been considered pieces of evidence to classify this grave as a "chariot burial", like the ones found at the tombs of Ur and Kish, which share similar issues as we will see. Some wood remains, interpreted as the only remains of the chariots, the space between the equid skeletons and the human body, as the wealth and numerous funerary goods present in the grave have been also borne as additional pieces of evidence supporting this interpretation (Killick & Roaf, 1979: 540). Further pathological analyses of both skeletons may help to corroborate this interpretation, but the identification of these individuals as donkeys or onagers (or even hybrids of both species) has not been possible to be determined (Killick & Roaf, 1979: 540; Vila, 2006: 116).

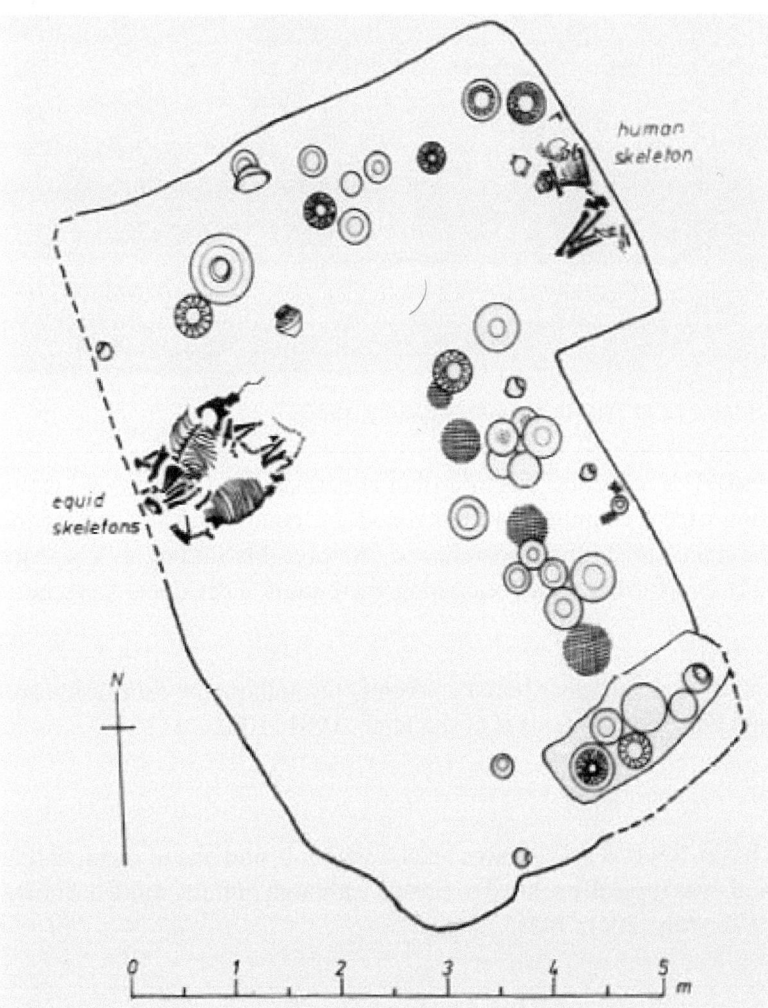

FIG. 10. TELL MADHHUR TOMB IN TRENCH 5G (AFTER KILLICK AND ROAF, 1979).

Finally, other two unidentified equids skeletons were found in a tomb of the early Akkadian period (Killick & Roaf, 1979: 540; Zarins, 1986: 173-174; Way, 2011: 143).

3. 2. 3. Uch Tepe (Tell Razuk)

This site is a triangular mound located in the Hamrin basin whose major period of occupation is dated to the Early Dynastic (Gibson et al., 1981: 28-29).

At this site, two articulated donkey skeletons placed side by side in prone position were found in a burial pit (*Locus 415, Burial 12*) (fig. 11) dating from early Akkadian period (ca. 2300 BC). This burial consisted of a large chamber that also contained a group of pottery vessels that seemed to form a functional unit, and several copper items including some weapons such as blades, daggers and axes (Zarins, 1986: 174; Philip, 1995: 149; Way, 2011: 143). However, the possibility of a chariot associated with the equids seems unlikely due to the position of the grave goods around the equids (Gibson et al., 1981: 73-74).

FIG. 11. BURIAL 12 AT TELL RAZUK (AFTER ZARINS, 1986).

This grave was connected by a tunnel to a smaller chamber that contained the fragmented human remains of a male. The association of the chamber that contained the equids and the rest of the funerary goods to the grave of the man has led the researches to interpret this finding as a warrior burial (Gibson et al., 1981: 73-74). No further data concerning the equids individuals have been provided.

The rest of the animal bones at this site were not distributed uniformly throughout the excavation and have been found in rubbish pits and domestic contexts (Gibson et al., 1981: 109).

3. 2. 4. Tell Abu Qasim

This site is located in the Hamrin basin. Several graves have been found in it, and one of them, dating from ED III or Old Akkadian Period, was typically related to equids, although nothing more is known about this finding (Zarins, 1986: 175; Way, 2011: 143).

3. 2. 5. Kish

Kish is located in central Iraq, around 15 km east of Babylon. Several famous "chariot burials" were excavated in the Y-trench (East Kish) at this site, all of them dating from ED II (ca. 2500). These tombs were formal structures with brick vaults associated to draft animals and vehicles, grave goods and even human attendants in some cases, as in the case of Ur, although skeletal remains have not been found in all of them (like in the case of *Burial IV*). *Burial I* contained human remains related to rein-rings, two chariot wheels and the remains of at least three bovids. *Burial II* contained four donkeys next to the remains of a four-wheeled vehicle (fig. 12). And *Burial III* was similar to *Burial I* since it also contained a copper rein-ring with the figure of an equid, three two-wheeled vehicles and the remains of several equids and bovids, although it has not been possible to determine how many of them were present at this burial (Zarins, 1986: 169-171; Way, 2011: 144-145). Concerning *Burial II*, although at first sight it is likely to think the animals and the vehicle were directly linked, Gibson has stated that the equids were probably related to a different undetected burial (Gibson, 1972: 85).

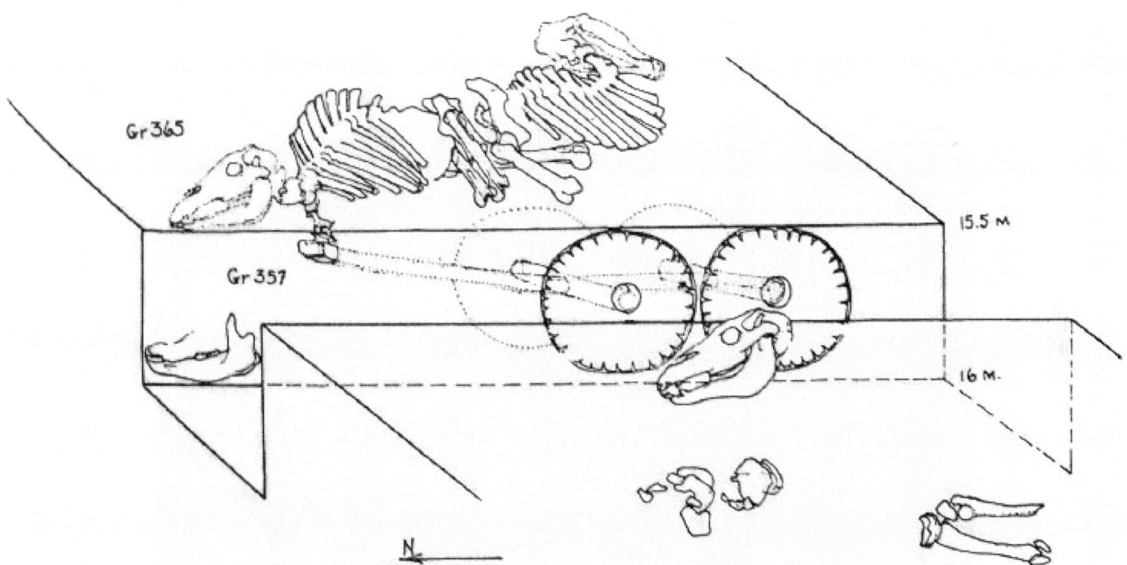

FIG. 12. A RECONSTRUCTION OF BURIAL II (AFTER ZARINS 1986).

3. 2. 6. Abu Salabikh

Several articulated skeletons were discovered in different contexts at this site, located 20 km northwest of ancient Nippur.

Equids

The first of them, an equid identified probably as an adult *kúnga* (Clutton-Brock, 1986: 209) and dating from the end of the ED III (2350 BC), was found in a deep ash-tip lying against the south-east face of an administrative building in Area E (fig.13). This equid was deposited in the rubbish lying on its right site looking north, and their bones were dark grey, which means it was exposed to heat and probably suggests this individual was trapped in a fire that occurred in the building where it was kept, although the fragmented condition of its skull led the researchers to think about a blow as the cause of its death, probably deliberated (Postgate, 1986: 202-204; Clutton-Brock, 1986: 209; Way, 2011: 145). Although this find does not seem at first of ritual nature, it must be borne in mind the symbolical importance of *kúnga*, and the presence of this individual in this building, possibly a temple or a palace, as it has been argued (Postgate, 1986: 201), may suggest it was in relation with the breeding of these hybrids, as in the case of the temple in Nagar (Syria).

Two other equid skeletons (fig. 14) were found in a funerary chamber (*Grave 162*) (fig. 15) dated to 2450 BC and placed behind the floor of a courtyard (Court 58) located south to the Area E and therefore within the administrative complex were the previous individual was discovered (Postgate,

1986: 201). They were lying side by side as if yoking together with their heads against the west end of the chamber looking north. Five ordinary conical bowls and a small rough triangle of copper were also found in this grave, as well as some organic remains, probably traces of meat offerings. Although the remains of any possible vehicle associated with these equids has not survived, this find has been interpreted as a "chariot burial" due to the position of the equids and the resemblance of this discovery to other contemporary and similar ones such as the burials at Kish, considering these equids as funerary furnishing instead of meat or other purposes (Postgate, 1986: 201-202; Zarins, 1986: 171-172; Way, 2011: 145-146).

A second pair of equids was lately discovered behind the first two, as well as a fifth one south to them. None of these individuals found at graves have been identified, and direct human association has not been confirmed neither (Postgate, 1983: 96; Zarins, 1986: 172; Way, 2011: 146). What it has been presumed due to the presence of a small group of copper vessels found in the grave is that a human skeleton must have been somewhere at the centre (Postgate, 1983: 96-97).

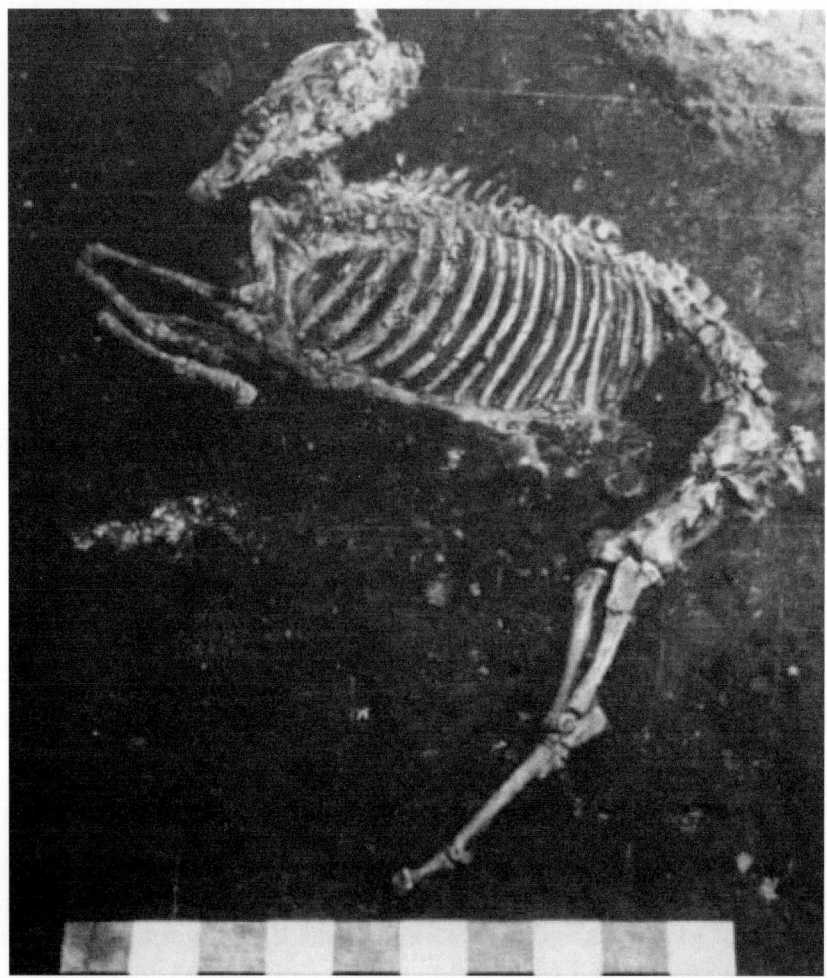

FIG. 13. ARTICULATED EQUID SKELETON FOUND IN ASH-TIP AT ABU SALABIKH (AFTER POSTGATE, 1986).

Ovicaprines

Some complete skeletons of young ovicaprines have been found among the funerary offerings in several graves, in most cases near to the rest of the disarticulated animal remains that usually constitute the grave offerings assemblages (Clutton-Brock, 1986: 207-208). Nevertheless, although these findings stand out from the rest of the discarded remains, not only from food debris but also from ritual or funerary contexts, further information is not provided and a detailed research about them has not been carried out.

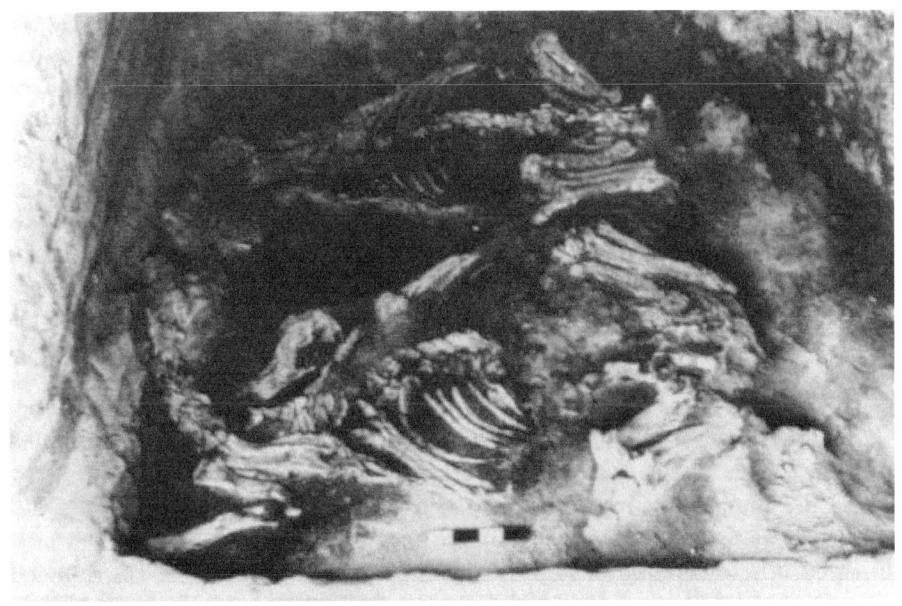

Fig. 14. Equids found at *Grave 162* (after Postgate, 1986).

Fig. 15 Plan of *Grave 162* showing the five equids in what have been considered their original position (after Postgate, 1983).

The rest of the animal bones found at this site were in a very fragmentary condition and they have been interpreted as food, associated with rubbish pits and domestic contexts (Clutton-Brock & Burleigh, 1978: 89-100), so I will not include further details about them in this paper.

3. 2. 7. Nippur

Several burials dated to the Early Dynastic IIIA were discovered at this site in the Levels XIV-X. Most of these burials were single interments located in open areas close to houses, but there is one that outstands from the rest of the burials, *Burial 14*, a three-phased sequence burial containing possibly three generations of adults of what can be interpreted as a family group. This burial was considerably more complex than the rest, consisting of several chambers that contained pottery vessels, jewelry and metal items as well as other objects, interpreted as social and identity markers of this elite group (McMahon, 2006: 37, 47-51). Several articulated animal skeletons were found in this burial associated with human remains (fig. 16).

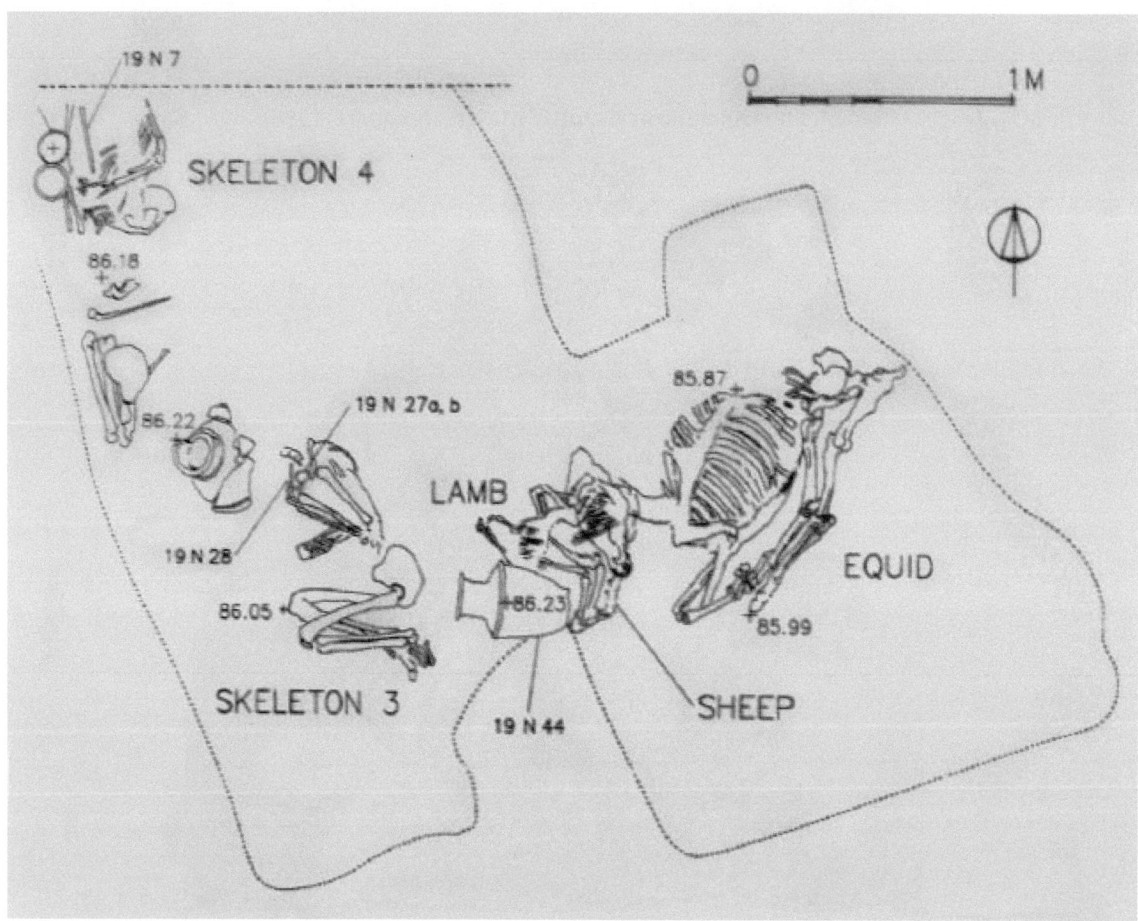

FIG. 16. PLAN OF *BURIAL 14*, LEVEL XIIIB CHAMBER (AFTER MCMAHON, 2006).

Equids

It seems that an equid (fig. 17) was buried with *skeleton 4* and/or *3* as the first burials in the chamber, with *skeleton 2* added subsequently. Although the equid appeared situated closer to *skeleton 3*, it has been stated that the association of weapons and other metal objects with *skeleton 4* leads us to think about him as the most likely candidate to be related to the equid (McMahon, 2006: 48). No further information about the skeleton of the animal is provided in the bibliography.

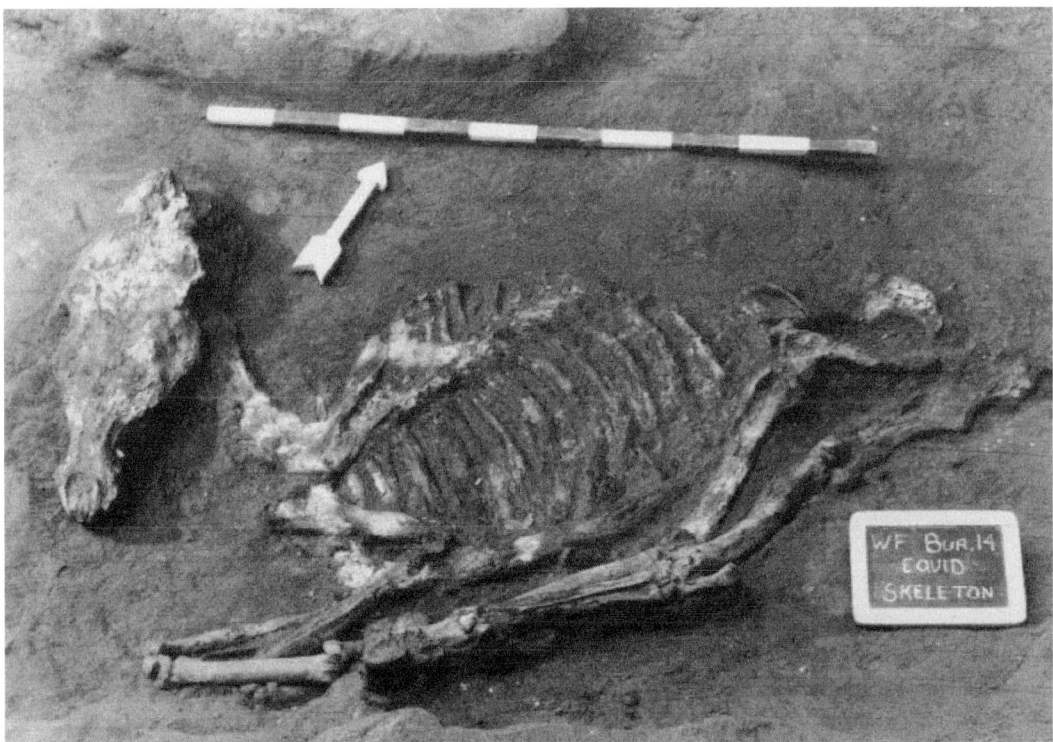

FIG. 17. EQUID SKELETON AT BURIAL 14 (AFTER MCMAHON, 2006).

Ovicaprines

Three ovicaprines–two adult sheep and one lamb–were piled between *skeletons 2* and *3*, partially above the equid previously described and probably associated with one of those two human individuals (fig. 18). The lowest sheep was lying on its right side with his forequarters heading north and with his head intentionally removed. This is due to a disturbance that took place in this burial when *skeleton 2* was interred in the structure, affecting the rest of the individuals (both humans and animals), as in the case of *skeleton 3*, for example, whose skull was also removed. The lamb was lying in the same position over this sheep's legs, and the third ovicaprine was separated of this pair by a thin layer of fill, with his head to the north but lying on its left side (McMahon, 2006: 47-48).

Since these individuals have been automatically interpreted as part of the assemblage of the funerary offerings (McMahon, 2006: 48-51), no further analyses and discussion have been carried out about them. Moreover, it is not clear why the reports provide so unequal information about the different animal skeletons despite most of them appeared to the same strata.

3. 2. 8. Lagash (Tell al-Hiba)

Lagash was once located northeast of the merge of Euphrates and Tigris rivers and southeast of Uruk, and it was one of the oldest cities of Sumer. A man was found buried south of the exterior wall of a large ED III building located in *Area C*. He was associated with an equid (fig. 19), later identified as an onager, and both were surrounded by several ceramic vessels (Littauer & Crouwel, 1979: 24: Zarins, 1986: 171; Way, 2011: 146-147).

3. 2. 9. Ur

Ancient Ur (now Tell al-Muqayyar) is located in southern Iraq, approximately 17 km west of Nasiriyah. Although nowadays the Euphrates runs east of the site, it curved southwest of it in ancient times (Baadsgaard et al., 2012: 127).

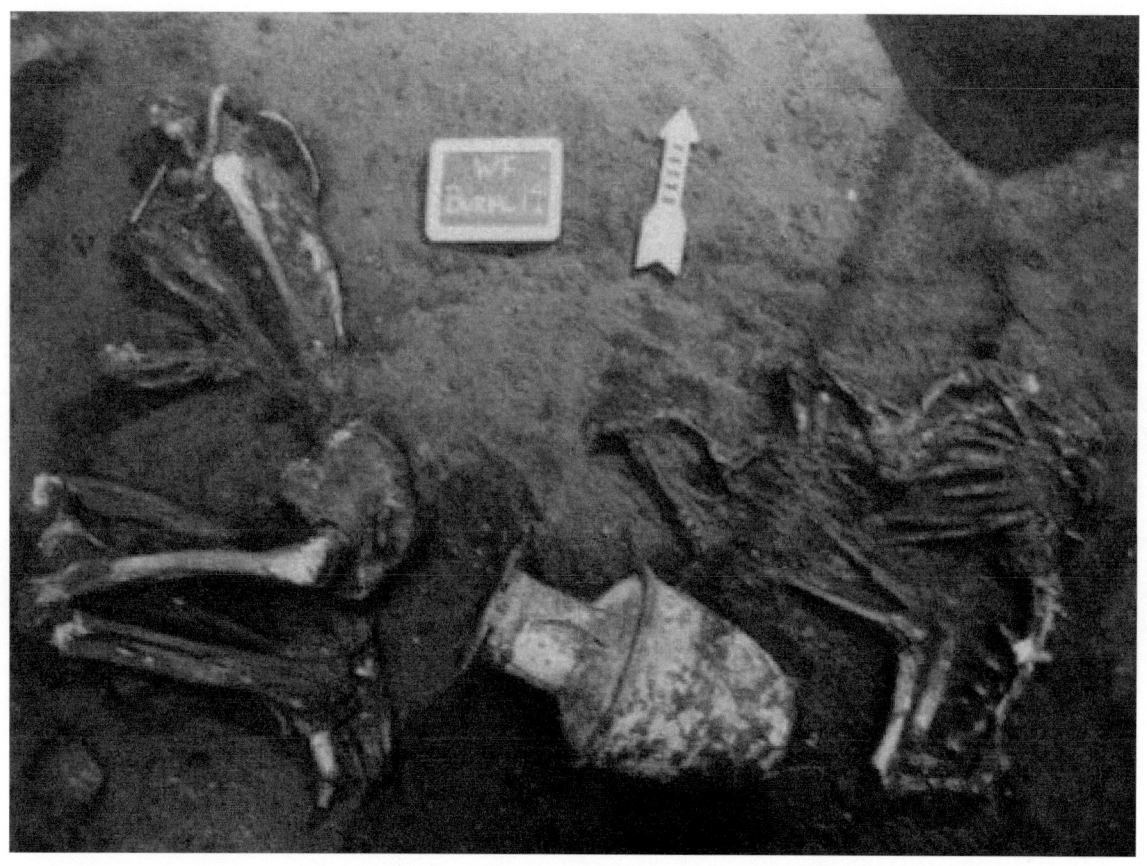

Fig. 18. Ovicaprine skeletons located next to skeleton 3 at Burial 14 (after McMahon, 2006).

Fig. 19. Articulated onager skeleton found at Lagash (Area C) (after Zarins 1986).

Several articulated animal skeletons have been found within some of the graves of the famous Royal Cemetery discovered more than seventy years ago by Sir Leonard Woolley. More than 2100 burials have been recorded and it has been estimated that originally there were around the double amount of them, but many have been destroyed by later disturbances. Most of the burials, that occurred over a long time, were simple inhumations consisting of a single body accompanied by a few grave goods, but 16 of all these tombs have been considered and denominated the "royal tombs" of Ur's kings and queens, dated to Early Dynastic IIIA (2600-2450 BC) (Wooley, 1934: 20-38; Baadsgaard et al., 2012: 127-128). From these tombs are the articulated animal remains that have been recorded at Ur, exactly from Graves (GP) 580, 789, 800 and 1232.

Grave *PG 580* contained four bovids associated with the traces of a vehicle and a copper rein-ring; other six bovids were discovered at *PG 789* (a.k.a. "The King's Grave") also related to a silver rein-ring with a bovid figure and two four-wheeled vehicles (fig. 20); *PG 800* ("queen Pu-abi's tomb") contained two bovids and a electrum rein-ring with an equid depicted (fig. 21); and finally, *PG 1232* contained several items including rein-rings, two chariot wheels and what have been identified as two donkeys. However, since Woolley identified at first the bovids from *PG 800* also as asses, the identification of these individuals, not preserved due to their bad condition, results suspect (Woolley, 1934: 46-53; Littauer & Crouwel, 1979: 25: Zarins, 1986: 166-168; Way, 2011: 147-148; Baadsgaard et al., 2012: 130-137).

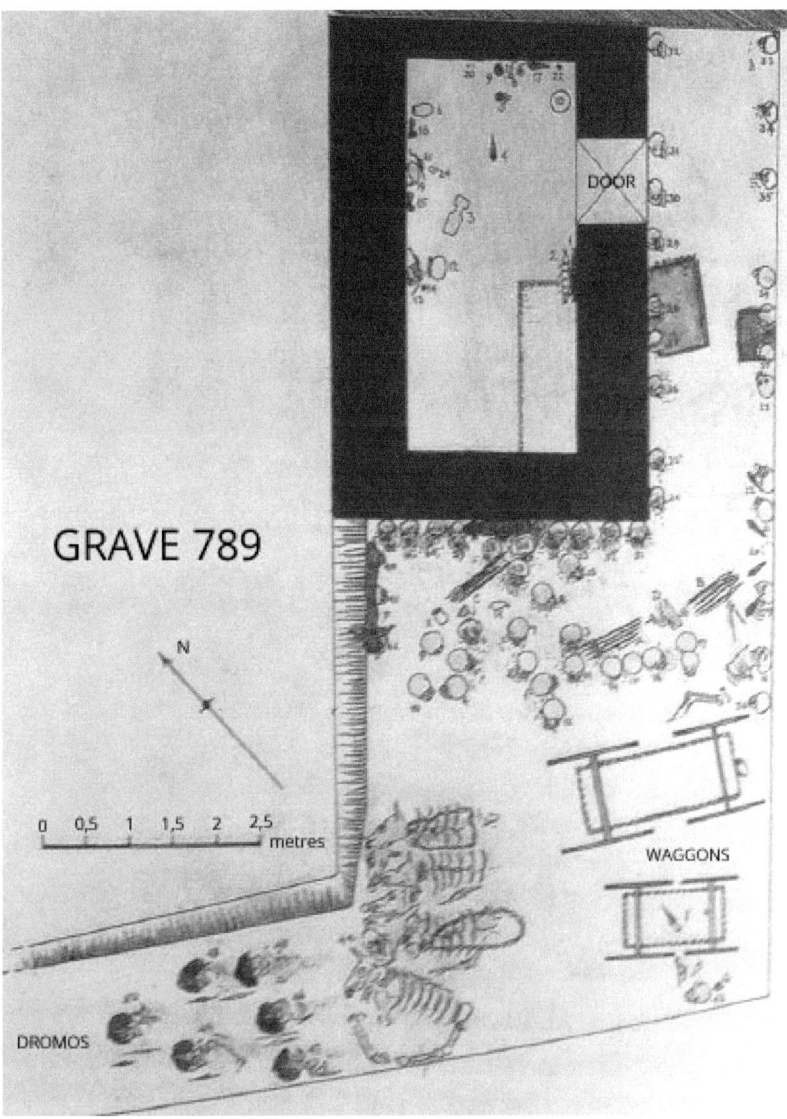

FIG. 20. PLAN OF *PG 789* (AFTER BAADSGAARD ET AL., 2012).

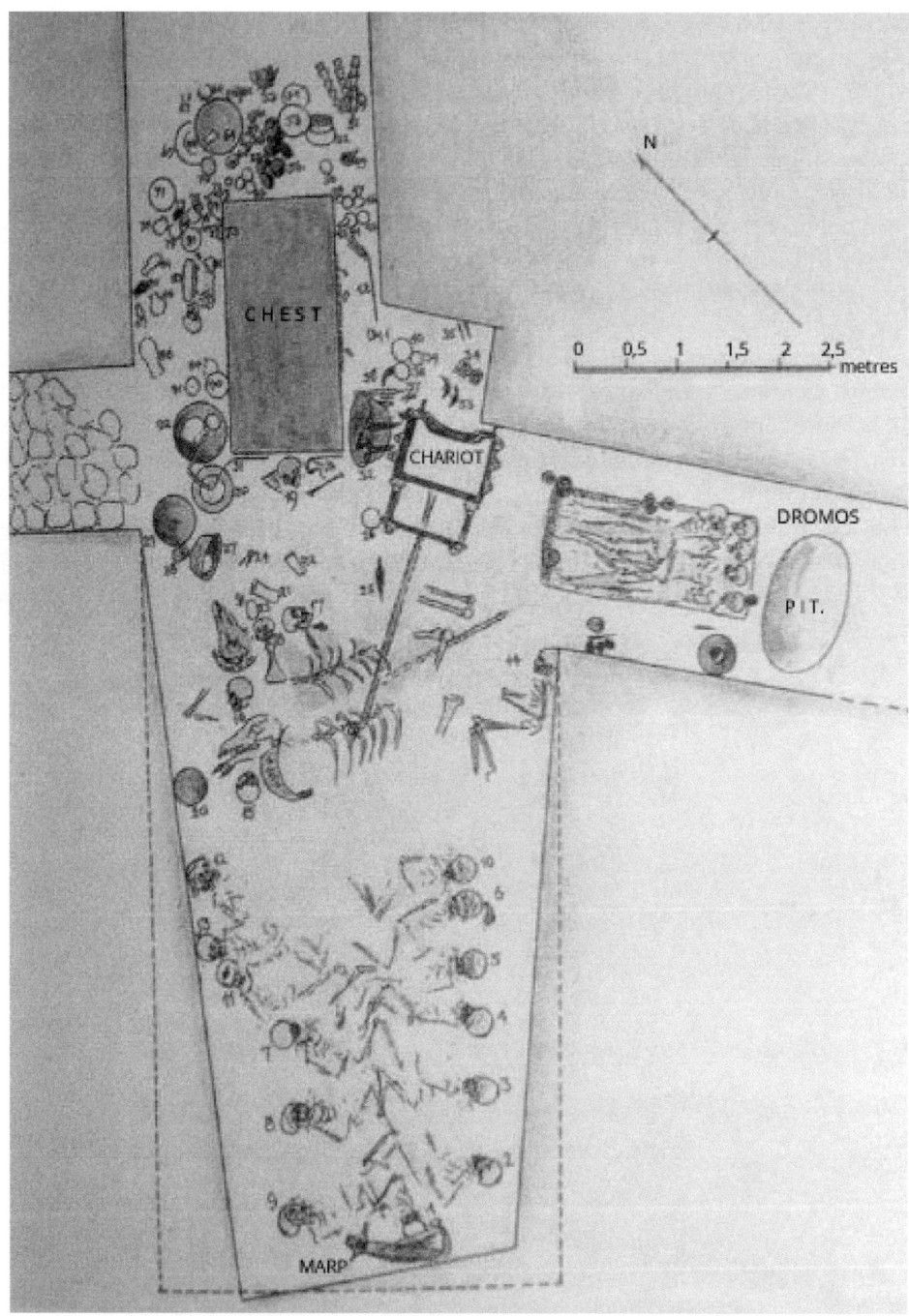

FIG. 21. PLAN OF *PG 800* (AFTER BAADSGAARD ET AL., 2012).

Due to their features, these burials have been identified and interpreted as chariot burials, as in some other cases such as Kish and Tell Madhhur. The role of animals in the contexts of these burials is open to discussion and not clear at all, as we will see in the discussion section. However, it is usually argued that they represent provisions for the dead, as well as offerings for netherworld deities in some cases, something supported by the written sources (Baadsgaard et al., 2012: 150). The case of the tombs of Ur is really illustrative and outstanding since the chariots have been preserved in some cases, as well as the animals, and the association of the former with the latter is clear to see.

3. 2. 10. Additional information about other sites

There are other animal assemblages mentioned in the bibliography which I decided not to describe in detail in this paper despite their similarity concerning features and context with other discussed sites. The reason is that in those cases the animal bones have been found in a fragmentary and disarticulated state or because they have been found in a place related to but out of the geographic area of this survey. However, I consider convenient at least to mention them.

Concerning Mesopotamia, these are the Kermanshah valley, where discarded remains have been recorded most from kitchen middens in several sites and caves, dating mainly from the Neolithic and the Chalcolithic (Bökönyi, 1977); Susa (central Iran), where several bovid individuals have been found related to chariots in mortuary contexts, although the remains have not been preserved (Zarins, 1986: 168-169); and Tell Asmar, where the animal remains came from general tell occupational debris and not from *in situ* articulated skeletons (Hilzheimer, 1941; Zarins, 1986: 179).

4. Structured deposition of animal remains in the Fertile Crescent during the II Millennium BC

While in the III Millennium BC animal burials, above all the ones called "chariot burials", were plentiful in Syria and Mesopotamia and constituted the main type of structured deposition of animal bones, there was no evidence about this practice in the Levant. Surprisingly, the opposite scenario occurs in the II Millennium BC, where we find only a few cases in Syria and Mesopotamia while most of them appear in the Levant, which is the main area where this phenomenon takes place during this period. However, part of the Mesopotamian pattern could be simply due to the fact that there were fewer excavation data from the II Millennium BC than from the III. Indeed, only two sites from Mesopotamia and one from Syria are explained in this section. Thus, this should be borne in mind at the time of interpreting the data from historical and cultural viewpoints. The quandary of the data has been already previously stated in this paper.

It has been stated that animal burials–also the main type of structured animal deposition in this period–as they occur in the II Millennium BC, at least concerning equids, are a continuation of the tradition of the previous millennium (Way, 2010: 211). However, to what extent can this be claimed? If most of the articulated animal remains found at the Levant display cultural continuity with those from the Egyptian Delta, Syria and Mesopotamia, why there is no evidence of such practices in the previous millennium? Hence, at what extent could we state that populations from the Levant adopted such practices at the time when in Mesopotamia and Syria were disappearing? Is it something related to an increase of social complexity that took place in the Euphrates Valley in the third millennium BC and occurs now in the Levant?

The animal remains found in this millennium are also usually attested related to human tombs as it happens in previous periods, but some of them have been found in *loculi* burials and sometimes with no connection to human remains (or anything in general). However, unlike it happens in Syria and Mesopotamia in previous millennia, the finding of complete ovicaprine skeletons in Middle Bronze cultic contexts (MBII above all) is a trend that occurs in tomb and temple contexts (Klenck, 2002: 22). It is worth of mention how donkey burials are unknown in the Iron Age, as it has been pointed out (Lev-Tov, 2006: 209).

4. 1. Structured deposition of animal remains in Mesopotamia during the II Millennium BC

Articulated animal skeletons in this period have been found only in two sites: Tell Ababra, where a 'chariot burial' is recoded, although the information available is really limited; and Isin, where a dog cemetery related to a healing Mesopotamian goddess has been found.

4. 1. 1. Tell Ababra

This site is located in the Hamrin basin. Four graves with equids remains dated to the Old Babylonian period (ca. 1700 BC) were discovered at Tell III, although only the equids from *Grave 29* have been analysed, identified as an adult male donkey (Driesch & Amberger, 1981: 67-70; Zarins, 1986: 176; Way, 2011: 143). Woefully, there is no more detailed information about this site.

4. 1. 2. Isin

In this site, located in southern Mesopotamia, 33 dog burials dated to 1000 BC were found in a ramp leading to the temple of Gula, goddess of healing. In this temple, called the "House of the Dog", numerous votive plaques and clay figurines depicting dogs were also found (Collins, 1990: 225; Hesse & Wapnish, 2008: 560, 567). It is known through the texts and the iconography from the second and first millennia BC that dog was associated to this goddess, probably due to its presumed medical qualities, and the burials may suggest the existence of rituals of healing dedicated to the cult of this goddess to which dogs were linked (Collins, 1990: 225: Hesse & Wapnish, 2008: 560).

Dogs were placed in shallow pit graves and then covered with soil. Of the total amount of 33 dogs, 16 were puppies, 6 young adults and 10 adults, being one of them missing. Osteological analyses reflect that they were unmanaged and died naturally since more than the half of both the young adults and the adults have either missing teeth and/or fractures in limbs and feet that seem to have healed by the time of the animal's death (Hesse & Wapnish, 2008: 560, 567). It has been stated that in these circumstances these buried dogs are not distinguishable from unmanaged urban dogs and therefore they did not have to be specially treated in life, thus they were probably just kicked around (Hesse & Wapnish, 2008: 560). Further discussion about the dog burials at Isin will be work out in section 5.3.

4. 2. Structured deposition of animal remains in Syria during the II Millennium BC

Although animal remains have been recorded at several sites, only in Umm el-Marra, inhabited again after some centuries of abandonment, structure deposits of animal remains have been found, again in contexts of ritual activity.

4. 2. 1. Umm el-Marra

New ritual activity is evidenced at this site during this period since after more than a century of abandonment Umm el-Marra was reoccupied from ca. 1900 to 1600 BC. As a result of this new beginning a large stone platform of around 40 meters diameter (called *Monument 1*) was built above the zone of the third millennium tombs (see section 3). It is argued that this building worked as a vast circular stage involving large-scale ceremonial activities despite no evidence of a shrine or any structure has been found over the monument, although these structures might have been lately destroyed (Schwartz, 2013: 508-509). Following this logical discussion, *Monument 1*, occupying a central location, would have dominated the live of the population in the same way that the tomb complex of the III Millennium BC (see section 3) (Schwartz, 2013: 509-510).

In addition to *Monument 1*, the other data about the new ritual activity comes from a circular subterranean feature called *Shaft 1*, located in the south-central part of *Monument 1*. Inside this feature 11 layers of both human and animal skeletons have been found, carefully interred and separated by clean deposits of soil. This is suggestive of a ritualised behaviour due to the repetitiveness that can be stated in the deposition of these individuals, as it has been argued (Schwartz, 2013: 510).

In the first level located at the bottom of the shaft (level 11) were buried 13 human individuals (men, women and children) with no goods associated and placed between two layers of stones and boulders. The bodies presented blunt force trauma, an indicator of death by a blow to the head, and an adult dog was interred with them. In the rest of the layers, deposited above this first one, several animal skeletons of various animals of different species and age were found separated as well by homogeneous clay soil (table. 4) (Schwartz, 2013: 511-512).

Subterranean shafts containing ritual deposits are attested in several sites of Bronze Age Syria, but only in Umm el-Marra human remains have been found (Schwartz, 2013: 512). Thus, this event has been interpreted as a singular occurrence, resulted of a unique ritual event taking place in a time of severe stress as an extraordinary gesture to entreat the gods for assistance (Schwartz, 2013: 513).

Animal	Fetus	Sub-adults	Adults	Total
Equids	6	2	3	11
Dogs	0	1	5	6
Ovicaprines	1	2	0	3

TABLE. 4. AGE RATIO OF ANIMALS FOUND IN SHAFT 1 (AFTER SCHWARTZ, 2013).

4. 3. Structured deposition of animal remains in the Levant during the II Millennium BC

Most of the articulated animal remains found at the Levant come from sites located to the south, which has led scholars to consider this region to display cultural continuity with the Egyptian Delta (Way, 2011: 116). Although numerous donkey burials are attested, articulated remains of other animals are more frequent than in Mesopotamia and Syria not only in previous periods but also in contemporary ones.

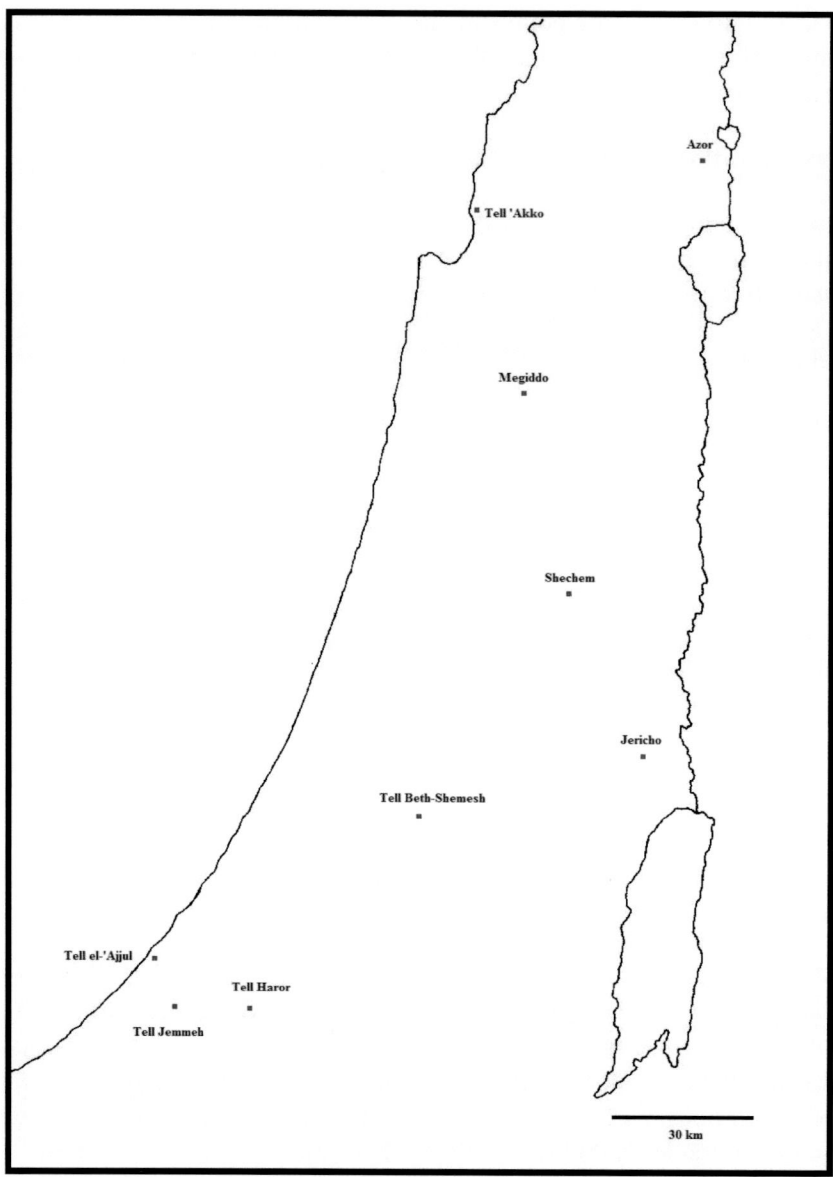

FIG. 22. SOME OF THE SITES DISCUSSED IN THIS SECTION (AUTHOR).

4. 3. 1. Azor

A particular burial cave was discovered in *Area B* during the excavations of Moshe Dothan that took place in 1958 and 1960 at this site, 6 km from Jaffa. This cave, dug in the Middle Bronze Age II, was used for human and equid burials since the beginning of Late Bronze Age to Iron Age I. Both human and equids were found in several layers lying side by side (Way, 2011: 118). A few additional animal remains have been also found in mortuary contexts, all of them discarded and fragmented although found *in situ*. Thus, they have been interpreted as funerary offerings and/or even social markers (Maher, 2012: 196-198).

4. 3. 2. Sasa

From Sasa, in Upper Galilee, several remains of ovicaprine, pig and bovid individual were found in two tombs dating from the Middle Bronze IIB and Middle Bronze IIA-C, respectively (Horwitz, 1987: 253). As it happened in Jebel Qa'aqir, a number of articulated bones were present, suggesting whole joints at the time of the deposition, although cranial remains were present at these tombs (Horwitz, 1987: 253-254).

4. 3. 3. Tell 'Akko

A complete donkey skeleton from the MB IIB period was discovered in 1983 in this site, located on the northern bank of the Na'aman River. Since it was found beneath a wall it has been interpreted as a foundation deposit, although the data concerning this finding is limited and not further details have been published (Way, 2011: 117).

4. 3. 4. Megiddo

The animal remains from this site have stirred up an intense discussion since a system of animal processing for which bovids and ovicaprines were positively selected for the sacrificial system has been argued (Wapnish & Hesse, 2000: 429, 448). However, animal bones were discarded. Although the animal remains obtained from tombs and occupation levels at this site are numerous but fragmentary, there are some data I consider convenient to set out.

The skeleton of a cow with the head missing was found related to *Tomb 903* (MB II) (fig. 23), where portions of canids and pig have been also found, as well as in several tombs of the same strata (Guy, 1938: 11-18). Equid remains were also found in *Tomb 1100*, dating from Middle Bronze Age II, together with fragmented ovicaprines remains, that were also found in tombs *911*, *912* and *989* (Klenck, 2002: 22). Thus, the scenario of Megiddo is similar to the rest of the contexts where articulated animal remains have been found.

FIG. 23. BOVID SKELETON FOUND IN TOMB 903 AT MEGIDDO (AFTER GUY, 1938).

4. 3. 5. Sidon

A partially complete and semi-articulated sheep skeleton was found at this site inside the grave of a female (*Burial 99*) dated to Middle Bronze IIA (fig. 24). This individual was deposited among other grave goods which included the discarded remains of another sheep and three fishes (Doument-Serhal, 2013: 86).

FIG. 24. SHEEP SKELETON IN *BURIAL 99*, SIDON
(AFTER DOUMENT-SERHAL, 2013).

4. 3. 6. Shechem

Two articulated animal skeletons have been found at this site, located in the present village of Balâtah, in the Palestinian West Bank.

The first of them is the skeleton of a small ovicaprine dated to the Middle Bronze Age IIB (1750-1650 BC) that was found buried under a stone-lined pit (fig. 25). This finding was located in the acropolis of the site in an area of human burials, but was unrelated to any of them. Since this individual was discovered laying on a bed of small stones it has been argued that a special significance may be given to it, although further discussion has not been carried out (Campbell, 2002: 29, 61).

The second skeleton is from an unidentified equid dated to the Late Bronze Age IIA (ca. 1400-1325 BC) yielded under a layer of debris beneath the floor of the gate of a tower guard room (fig. 26) (Campbell, 2002: 173-174; Way, 2011: 117). Although fully articulated, this individual has been found decapitated, and several interpretations have arisen. E. F. Campbell has pointed out that it is not possible at all to know if this individual is a casualty of the destruction that ended the stratum

Fig. 25. Ovicaprine skeleton found at Shechem in *Locus 6:18* in *Room 8* (after Campbell, 2002).

where it was found or if its represent some sort of sacrifice (Campbell, 2002: 173-74), while K. C. Way argues that a decapitation seems to be a strong indication of ritual activity, and talks about the possibility of this finding to be an illustrative example of a treaty ceremony (see section 5. 2) (Way, 2011: 118).

Fig. 26. Equid skeleton found at Shechem (after Campbell, 2002).

4. 3. 7. Jericho

This site, located at Tel es-Sultan, has been excavated in numerous times, being the campaign of D. Kenyon that took place from 1952 to 1958 the most known. Some articulated faunal remains have been recorded from the tombs of this site, from which faunal remains comprised mostly joints of mutton in mortuary contexts (Klenck, 2002: 22).

Equids

A total of 15 equids have been identified from the equid remains that have been yielded associated with tombs of the Middle Bronze Age IIB-C (Way, 2011: 118-119). In 7 of the tombs of the equids have been found in shaft-fills (in tombs *B48*, *B51*, *D22*, *J3*, *J37*, *M11* and *P21*), and in the other two they have been found in the tomb chamber (tombs *D9* and *B50*) (Way, 2011: 119). In general, the data is considerably limited and there is not enough information to know to what extent these individuals were found complete and/or articulated. There are only further details about *Tomb J3*, where 3 equids that appeared next to 3 small ruminants have been identified as donkey (Way, 2011: 119).

Ovicaprines

Some jointed ovicaprines individuals have been recorded in some of the tombs, usually accompanied by discarded remains of other animal species, most of them also ovicaprines. A total of 10 ovicaprines were found in a jointed or articulated state of preservation in five of the tombs, also from Middle Bronze Age IIB-C (tombs *G46*, *H6*, *H18*, *H22* and *G73*), most of them presenting traces of butchery and/or burning (Klenck, 2002: 22-23).

4. 3. 8. Gezer

This site was once a Canaanite city-state located in the foothills of the Judaean Mountains at the border of the Shfela region. Among the faunal remains recorded at the caves of this site two articulated animal skeletons have been found. One of them refers to a small bovid found in *Locus 3106* and dating from the Early Bronze IB (ca. 3100 BC) (Leger, 1988: 39). The other one consist of a donkey skeleton relatively complete and well preserved located in *Locus 10066* and dating from the Late Bronze IIA (ca. 1400 BC), whose remains suggest that the carcass was whole when deposited (fig. 27). Since its disposition indicates a deliberated dumping rather than an elaborated burial it has been argued that it might be used in construction activities and was dumped as part of the fill after being injured or dead (Leger & Zeder, 1988: 147).

FIG. 27. EQUID SKELETON FOUND AT *LOCUS 10066* (AFTER LEGER & ZEDER, 1988).

4. 3. 9. Tell Beth-Shemesh

The convoluted remains of a donkey were found in a circular pit dating from the Late Bronze Age-Iron Age transition. The back of this individual was broken in two places, one of them near the head. Due to that, this donkey has been considered the probable result of a treaty ceremony or of the neck-breaking ritual described in Exod 13:13, 34:20 (Way, 2011: 120-121).

4. 3. 10. Jebel Qa'aqir

At this site located west of Hebron eight tombs from the Middle Bronze Age I contained animal bones associated with human remains and a single tomb also contained animal bones but without human remains associated (Horwitz, 1987: 251). A total of 20 ovicaprines represented these bone assemblages, none of them adult. A high proportion of them were articulated, suggesting whole joints when deposited, although no cranial elements were present (Horwitz, 1987: 252).

4. 3. 11. Tell el-'Ajjul

This site, located on the northern bank of the Besor River, was excavated in the early 1930s, where diverse equid burials were revealed. Few measurements were given in the reports and most of the bones were not saved, thus the material was unable to be properly analysed (Way, 2011: 121-122). Most of the equids date to the Middle Bronze Age and are incomplete, with the exception of *Tomb 1417* (MB IIA), where a complete skeleton of an equid identified as a donkey was found in a chamber that contained a single warrior burial (Klenck, 2002: 22; Way, 2011: 122-126). With the exception of *Pit 1504*, interpreted as a foundation deposit (Way, 2011: 122-123), all of the equids remains are related to human remains. M. Murray suggested in the reports of the 1950s that these equid remains were the evidence of Hyksos sacrificial feast that involved the dismemberment and burning of these animals (Mackay & Murray, 1952: 33). Although the interpretation of these remains as a result of ceremonial sacrifices fits correctly the archaeological evidence, the Hyksos hypothesis has been nowadays abandoned since animal ritual and burial have been attested all over several millennia in a wide variety of sites all over the Near East.

4. 3. 12. Tell Jemmeh

In 1978 a neonatal equid skeleton was discovered in a pit beneath a wall at this site, located on the southern bank of the Besor River and south to Tell el-'Ajjul. The building and the pit date to Middle Bronze IIB, and the equid, which specie cannot be determined due to its youngness, was deposited in natural sitting position (Wapnish, 1997: 337-343: Way, 2011: 127-128). Due to its features, this finding has been interpreted as a foundation deposit.

4. 3. 13. Tel Haror

Tel Haror is located in the northern bank of Nahal Gerar. At this site, larger amounts of animal remains have been recorded. Structured deposits of animal remains have been found in the strata V-IV (Middle Bronze Age IIB-C) of the sacred complex of *Area K*, which includes a *migdal* temple, several enclosed spaces and courtyards (Katz, 2000: 43-61: Klenck, 2002: 31-34: Way, 2011: 129-130).

Two intact donkey individuals were found on the floor of the chamber of a donkey burial structure (*structure 8624*) behind a fill containing many disarticulated animal bones (including donkey) (Katz, 2000: 118: Klenck, 2002: 32: Way, 2011: 130-131). This building was a monumental domed mudbrick structure consisting of a narrow entrance leading to a circular chamber of 3.5 m of diameter (Katz, 2000: 49: Way, 2011: 130). The monumental nature of this structure had led the researchers to consider it an object of ongoing veneration that has no parallel neither in Egypt nor in the Levant (Way, 2011: 131).

Hundreds of dog and corvid bone remains have been also found in the *loculi* of *stratum V* the *Area K* sacred complex, most of them disarticulated or semi-articulated and deposited in contorted positions, being common among the dogs to have their head or torsos turned (Klenck, 2002: 68-73). However, some of them have been recorded articulated and in a better state of preservation. Thus, since the osteological features and the contexts of almost all of these individuals are similar or even the same the state of preservation or the level of articulation does not necessarily affect their nature and/or interpretation. Indeed, all the articulated individuals appeared along with layers of disarticulated remains of their same species in most cases, as it happens with the donkey remains. In the particular case of corvids and dogs they were usually deposited together.

From the articulated ones, it is worth standing out two corvid skeletons deposited in pits found in *loculi* 8430, as well as two dogs found in the same *loculi* that were deposited in a contorted and/or unnatural position (fig. 28, 29 and 30) (Klenck, 2002: 70). All of the dogs were puppies of less than six months of age (Klenck, 2002: 73).

FIG. 28. RAVEN SKELETON FOUND AT *LOCULI 8430/82091* AT TEL HAROR, ASSOCIATED WITH THE MANDIBLE OF A LAMB (AFTER KLENCK, 2002).

4. 3. 14. Additional information about other sites

As well as in the previous section, there are some sites I consider convenient to mention despite not having explained them in detail. These are Tel Miqne-Ekron, where a burial pit (*Locus 37041*) dating from Iron Age IB contained the disarticulated remains of several donkeys, associated with human burials, thus being considered a continuation of the equid burial traditions of the previous millennia (Lev-Tov, 2006: 208-209; Way, 2011: 120); and Lachish, where larger amounts of animal bone fragments, including equids, ovicaprines and bovids, have been yielded associated with cultic places dated to the second millennium BC (Croft, 2004: 2320-2345).

FIG. 29. ARTICULATED PUPPY SKELETON FOUND IN *LOCULI 8430/82443* AT TEL HAROR (AFTER KLENCK, 2002).

FIG. 30. ARTICULATED SKELETON OF A JUVELINE DOG ASSOCIATED WITH THE FRAGMENTED REMAINS OF A RAVEN AT TEL HAROR (AFTER KLENCK, 2002).

5. Discussion

This section is divided in four parts. In the first one I will develop the classification of the findings according to their interpretation and context. The second consists of the discussion itself, followed by a more detailed section regarding aspects about ritual and sacrifice. And last but not least, the conclusions.

5.1. Classification of the explained evidence

Most of the structured deposits of animal remains in the third millennium BC appeared in Syria and Mesopotamia, featured by donkey burials usually associated with elite human graves. The presence of ovicaprines and other animals within the tombs as offerings is also a common phenomenon, but the number of articulated individuals recorded is meaningfully fewer. It seems that all of the articulated animal deposits are attested in ritual and/or funerary contexts, which explains their carefully deposition that resulted in the good state of preservation of these kind of findings.

As I have remarked previously in this paper, structured animal deposits seem to constitute a united tradition in all Near East whose differences seem to increase throughout the time and the space. Nevertheless, it prevails in several ways even up to Hellenistic times since animal burial and offering are still present in the archaeological record, although displaying similar patterns. Animal rituals of offering and appeasement, associated or not with funerary contexts, persist in time with similar frequency. However, donkey burials decline in time whereas dog burials increase, above all among Mediterranean cultures. Hence, cultural continuity definitely seems to happen but with an increase of regional and cultural particularities.

Once the archaeological evidence has been explained I will draw up a classification of the findings according to their features and context as it is one of the aims of this paper. The categories stated are: animal burials inside human graves; animal burials related to human graves; animal burials unrelated to human graves; animals in sacred/ritual contexts; foundation deposits; and animal remains in non-ritual contexts. It must be borne in mind that these categories are not mutually exclusive and sometimes they can easily overlap, as we will see.

It is remarkable that no patterns of orientation neither position have been attested among the animal burials, not even in the cases of 'chariot burials' of the same site and period.

Animal burials inside human graves

Animals interred inside a human grave may be usually interpreted as symbolic markers of prestige and status of the deceased, as well as funerary furnishings. This depends on the animal, but it seems it is the case of what has been called 'chariot burials', and hence applicable at least for sure to both equids and bovids. Previous to the domestication of the donkey, bovids were the main burden beast and had a strong ideological significance resulting of their economic importance, being a symbol of fertility and power. But equids (above all donkeys, as we will see in the next section) hold a very special status and were animals of singular importance, mediating a special symbolic role that even bovids did not fulfil (Way, 2010: 211-212). 'Chariot burials' constitute an illustrative witness of this, where both equids and bovids were related to the elite graves as social markers and goods to employ in the afterlife, as detailed in cases such as Umm el-Marra (see section 3). This interpretation is supported by the fact that they were usually surrounded by the rest of the funerary goods. In some cases these goods even make reference to the animals interred, as the equids and bovids depicted in the rein-rings associated with the animals found in some 'chariot burials' as Kish or Nippur.

However, in the case of other animals (ovicaprines, dogs, pigs and even birds) found inside graves that display different features the interpretation might be different, as it will be explained in detail afterwards. These animals are susceptible of playing a role in the funerary ceremonies as sacrificial offerings and/ or food, although in some cases the same interpretation can be applied to bovids and equids interred in elite graves. This interpretation is especially appealing if the remains at issue are not complete (as for example concerning beheaded individuals as the cow at *Tomb 903* at Megiddo) or it exhibit cut marks. In some sites as Umm el-Marra, for example, equids have been deliberately killed and then interred as the rest of the equids interpreted as social markers and grave goods, even in the same spaces. Hence, animals interred inside a human grave, sacrificed or not, could play several roles in the same funerary rituals, as well as their inclusion within the tomb may imply several meanings simultaneously.

This type of finding is attested in all the geographic areas and studied in this paper. In the Levant we found animals interred inside human graves in the burial caves of Azor, the equid burial at Tell el-'Ajjul, as well as in Jericho and Sasa, where mainly ovicaprines have been found. Concerning Syria it may be included the equid and ovicaprines individuals found in the 'chariot burial' of Tel Halawa, as well as the bird species found at Tell Beydar. Finally, the most illustrative cases lie in the 'chariot burials' found at Mesopotamia in the sites of Tell Madhhur, Kish and Ur, which is probably the most noteworthy of them, without leaving behind Lagash and Nippur.

Animal burials related to human graves

There are not only a few cases where animal remains have been found outside a human grave but related to it. The interpretation of these cases is a bit more controversial, although the same interpretations that have been argued concerning animals found inside human graves can be applied to these cases in most of the occasions. Sometimes they can be interred apart due to a lack of space, but in other it seems deliberated. However, the differences with the first group previously stated seem not to be great. The fact that they are placed outside the tomb might lead us to think they played a different role in the funerary ceremonies, or that their purposes inside the grave were more restricted than in other cases. Anyway, in both cases, animals appear usually surrounded by other funerary goods as well as the remains of the ritual feastings.

The most striking cases of findings of this kind are attested undoubtedly in Syria, in the complex of Umm el-Marra, and secondly in Tall Bi'a. The tradition of animal burial related to human graves seems to continue from the third to the second millennium BC in this region as it can be implied from the burial of Tell Ababra. This practice is attested in the Levant also in Jericho and Tell el-'Ajjul, as well as in Megiddo (*Tomb 903*, previously mentioned) and Jebel Qa'aqir. Concerning Mesopotamia I may include the equid burials at Uch Tepe and al-'Usiyah, also considerably illustrative.

Animal deposits unrelated to human graves

It is difficult to make a distinction between animal burials and ritual deposits since burials usually take place in sacred spaces. In most of the cases both types may overlap, and the term 'burial' should be understood not only as a deliberated ritual deposition. As it has been stated (Porter, 2002a: 156), death carries strong ideological and social meaning, embodying simultaneously complex representations of society, world views and religious beliefs, representations produced through the mortuary practices.

Animal 'burials' non-related to human graves are normally identified as pits of deposits, but they are generally quite diverse. They are also attested in the three regions discussed in this paper, featured by the dog cemetery at Isin. We may also include the equid found beneath the administrative building at Abu Salabikh, which differs from the equids found in the funerary chamber, as well as the equid found at Abu Hamad, in Syria. In the Levant we may include the ovicaprine buried with no animal or human direct connection, and the cases of the equid burial complex at Tell el-'Ajjul.

Animals in sacred/ritual contexts

Some skeletal remains have been found associated to temples and/or sacred facilities. In such cases, the animal individuals appear usually surrounded by valuable objects and discarded animal bones, and displaying some anatomical issues (wrecked necks and/or backs, beheading, etc.). Although findings of this kind are diverse and in some case they can be considered also burials, as stated before, they are usually interpreted as the result of cultic ceremonies and rituals. This type refers to several sites at Syria and the Levant. *Shaft 1* at Umm el-Marra and the sacred complex at Tell Brak (see section 3) are undoubtedly the most striking and illustrative cases of this kind of findings. Some puppy deposits associated to the equid tombs of Umm el-Marra from the third millennium BC, as well as the bovid recorded at this site, might fit this category. Dog and corvid remains at Tell Haror, considered a witness of ritual ceremonies that I will further describe in detail, constitute also another illustrative case. Finally, the sheep found at Shechem fits also in this type of finding.

Foundation deposits

Animals located beneath walls and/or buildings have been usually interpreted as foundation deposits, whose ritual nature is deducted by the fact that equids–the only animal attested associated to this practice–appear usually articulated but incomplete, which suggests sacrifice. Further osteological analyses may help to support this interpretation.

This practice is attested in Syria in the third millennium BC in the cases of Umm el-Marra, where some equids found behind stone foundations of houses, and Tell Banat. On the other hand, it has been attested in the Levant during the second millennium BC in Tell Akko, Tell el-'Ajjul and Tell Jemmeh.

Animal remains in non-ritual contexts

There are some skeletal remains which have been interpreted as ritual deposits although they have been found in contexts that are not necessarily of ritual kind. In this category I shall include the sheep found under a stone-lined pit at Shechem (considered a ritual killing since it is beheaded) and the donkey found at Tell Beth-Shemesh.

5. 2. Analysis and interpretation of taxa

Animal bones yielded from non-domestic contexts are usually difficult to interpret since bones that have been deposited by chance must be distinguished from the remains of food offerings or sacrifices placed in tombs and/or sacred spaces. This task is especially important as it can provide information not only about economic issues but about ancient burial and ritual practices (Horwitz, 1987: 251). Anyway, when animals are carefully deposited we may reject the possibility that they were discarded as simple trash.

E. Vila argues that equids–for the most donkeys–began to be buried in association with humans in the third millennium BC, thus receiving a previously unknown treatment (Vila, 2006: 101). Since the interpretation of equid burials is diverse, it is likely to think that this special treatment is something applicable to the rest of the animals that appear also buried, and not only in funerary contexts but also in ritual and/or sacred ones. Thus, most of the structured deposits of animal remains from the third and second millennia BC are suitable of receiving such treatment. After all, the deliberate burial of whole animals is a rare find generally considered to show some kind of close relationship between man and animal, as well as the wearing of animal bits and art depiction of animals (Davis, 1987: 145). As E. Vila points out on the subject of the equids, this special treatment may be related to the domestication of such animal species, as I will develop afterwards in this section. In his own words, and relating to animal burials, since the inhumation of wild animals in human funerary contexts is an extremely rare phenomenon, the inclusion of sacrificed animals in human graves may suggest these animals were close to the human sphere, being domesticated or at least tamed (Vila, 2006: 116). This should be considered also in the case of animals in ritual contexts of other kind.

5. 2. 1. *Equids*

Equids appear mostly in ritual and/or funerary contexts usually associated to 'chariot burials'. According to E. Vila, the presence of equids in burials is indicative of a new relationship between humans and these animals, linked to their domestication, at the same time it means a different and uncommon significance of equids in comparison with other animals (Vila, 2006: 116).

In addition, he also develops what in my opinion is a really interesting and correct observation. Equids (either donkey or hybrids) can appear teamed and related to harnesses and/or carts, or aversely by their own. This can help us to understand the significance of these animals according to how they looked upon their owners, as well as to know better the meaning of their burials. While a group of equids related to a chariot may constitute the symbol of power of a warrior as well as an elite marker, a single buried equid is suggestive of the wealth of the owner. In both cases, the equids are aimed to serve their owners in the afterlife and the distinctive value of these animals is expressed, a value whose origins can be traced in the domestication of these species in the Ancient Near East (Villa, 2006: 117).

Each equid specie had a different use and significance, although in general all of them played an important role not only as burden animals but also as providers of secondary products. Equid hides were valued, and dogs were fed on the meat of equids (Clutton-Brock, 1986: 208).

Donkey

Donkey, present in Sumer at least since late IV Millennium BC according to cuneiform texts (Postgate, 1986: 201), was the common agricultural draught animal in the Ancient Near East (Postgate, 1986: 194, 200). Its domestication was part of what Sherrat has called "the revolution of the secondary products" (Milevski, 2011: 179). Donkey was used mainly as a pack animal and for plowing. The high adaptability of donkeys to arid climates and their skill to carry heavy loads over long distances repeatedly made the transportation of commodities easier, as well as it provided an easier access to material sources difficult to reach–such as copper–, which probably meant a reduction of the costs of these materials. Furthermore, the domestication of these animals allowed pastoralist to move further and more and even to transport their households, hence, allowing large-scale food redistribution and expanding overland trade (Grigson, 2006: 233; Milevski, 2011: 191).

Due to the impact of its domestication in society and economy the donkey achieved a high and multi-faced level of ideological significance. The presence of donkey remains in both religious and funerary contexts imply they had a special status in both life and death ceremonies and a high ideological significance. We know by the archaeological record that donkeys were highly valued and related to royal household, due to their impact and importance for economy and overland transport, as it can be inferred from their presence in elite cemeteries (Vila 2002: 116; Hesse et al. 2012: 228). They were also associated with divination, socio-economic status and even death in Syria, Mesopotamia, Egypt, Anatolia and the Levant since the Sumerian period to biblical times and far beyond (Way, 2011: 199).

The use of the donkey as mount for the royalty and their association with the elite is widely attested in the written sources since Akkadian times (Way, 2011: 73-74). In a letter of Bahdi-Lim, governor of Mari, to his king Zimri-Lim, he gives advice to the king concerning the proper means of transportation in public appearances and/or ceremonies, and the talks about the donkey as the proper animal for it. He even states that riding a donkey is the way to honor this kingship and presenting himself properly, what can tell us a lot about the significance of donkey and its relation to royalty (Way, 2011: 82-86). Concerning the horse, since it was lately the main animal for transportation activities, Way argues that although it was domesticated by this time (ca. 1700 BC) it was not yet associated with kingship, as it were the donkey, the mule or the *kúnga* (Way, 2011: 83). Donkey was also associated with the cult personnel since they were people of high social status equally (Way, 2011: 87).

As we could previously see, donkey burial is a well attested phenomenon and not only from the archaeological point of view since it is related in textual sources as the *Death of Gilgamesh* (Zarins, 1986: 180). Donkey, used as the proper way of royal transport, as displayed before, was interred in 'warrior burials' as both social markers and funerary furnishing among other purposes, as previously discussed. According to cuneiform texts, donkey seem to be listed in teams of four, which suggests a more elaborate instrument that a seed-plough controlled by a single man (Postgate, 1986: 200). Donkey burials are interesting since the osteological record of equids during the Bronze Age is low. We may think that dead donkeys were abandoned in the deserts and all over the trade routes since they did not belong to the household economy as the rest of the species.

Donkey burials are first attested in Egypt in sites as Abydos and Tarkhan and date from the beginning of the third millennium BC (Way, 2010: 211), appearing later in Mesopotamia and Syria. These first cases have been classified as 'chariot burials' since donkeys usually appear related to draft implements and other grave goods, as in the cases of Kish and Ur. Donkey burials grow diverse in time, and as it has been previously stated in this paper (see section 4), cultural continuity seems to have existed between Syria/Mesopotamia and the Levant in the second millennium BC (Way, 2010: 211), something applicable to most of the ritual deposits and animal burials explained in this survey. Finally, I should remark that the various contexts of the donkey burials emphasize that the perfomances of these burials were attended by different scripts with regard to motivation and the significance of the act for the individuals involved in its performance and the society for hose behalf it was done (Hesse et al., 2012: 228).

Further information about the socio-ideological significance of the donkey and the phenomenon of donkey burials can be found in the written sources. It is known that in the Sumerian culture donkeys hold symbolic and ceremonial connotations. In the Gudea Cylinders from the end of the third millennium BC donkey is represented as a symbol of the ruler and as a good work animal. It is also stated that donkeys were placed in the temple precincts and were designed to transport the deity on his ritual journeys due to his speed (Way, 2011: 92-94). In the hymnic text that describes the burial of Ur-Namma (establisher of the Third Dynasty of Ur and king from 2112 to 2095 BC) donkeys and chariots are deposited within the tombs as gifts to the netherworld deities. The use of donkeys as presents for local deities is attested in other texts, as in the case of the foundation tablets from Tell al-Mada, also where is stated that temples (as the one at issue, the temple of E-mus in Pa-tibira, built during the kingdom for En-metena from ca. 2700 to 2350 BC) worked as breeding centers for equids of high value (Way, 2011: 95-97). In addition, it is well known in both Akkadian and Hittite texts that donkey was also used in the "scapegoats" rituals, where it was consider a bearer of impurity (Way, 2011: 72). This symbolic role in this kind of rituals does not surprise to K. Way, who stated that since the donkey was the ultimate beast of burden in the ancient world it is logical that it was used in a ritual that needs something to be burden by an animal (Way, 2011: 72). However, if so, other burden animals with an important significance as the ox would be likely to participate in this kind of rituals, and there are other animals (as the dog, for example) that were also used in this rituals playing the same roles and are not related to burden activities. I personally feel that the role of the donkey as a burden beast might be one of the factors that led ancient populations to use it in this kind of rituals, but not the main one.

According to numerous Akkadian texts from Mari, the sacrifice of a donkey, that could even have been bought exclusively to be killed for the occasion, was usually part of treaty ceremonies among the Amorites. In this context, the killing of the animal was a symbol of the fate that would follow the party that dare to break the terms of the deal. At the same time, this kind of ceremonies were usually enacted in the presence of a deity, as it can be deducted from the occasional mention of temples and gods in them. Drinking and exchanging gifts are other parts of this kind of ceremonies (Way, 2011: 75-80, 200). It is likely to think that the deity was named also in order to work as a witness of the deal, a way to assure its compliance by the different parts of it. This kind of rituals has been presumably identified in some cases where donkeys appear isolated and displaying osteological issues. In the previous section we have referred to the individuals found at Tell Akko, Tell Beth-Shemesh and Tel Haror, where dogs and even corvids seem to have taken place in such practices.

Mule

Old Akkadian texts mention that mules (donkey-horse hybrid) were bred in the third millennium BC and they cost significantly more than donkeys, up to seven times more expensive, and having enough significance to be even interred related to human tombs (Zarins, 1986: 183-187). Maybe some of the unidentified equids found at 'chariot burials' in Syria and/or Mesopotamia were mules instead of donkeys or *kúnga*.

Onager

Unlike the donkey, that was not consumed as food but exceptional occasions such as ceremonial feasts or desperate circumstances (Way, 2011: 202), the onager was used for consumption. There is no evidence for its domestication, although we know they were kept for the breeding of hybrids (*kúnga*) and usually hunted for their meat and their hide (Postgate, 1986: 194, 199; Zarins, 1986: 187-188). Thus, how can we explain their presence in some burials, as in the case of Lagash? Were they consumed in funerary ceremonies or had they more significance than it seems through the archaeological record and the textual evidence?

Kúnga

According to Syro-Mesopotamian texts dating on 2600-2000 BC, the *kúnga* was a special type of equid resulting of the crossing between an onager and a donkey, the preferred one for pulling of wheeled vehicles, especially battle wagons. That is because the *kúnga* was stronger and faster than both the donkey and the onager. In fact, in the third millennium BC it was the animal that was aimed to draw the chariots of gods, officials and kings, according to the written sources. This animal was highly esteemed and basically preceded the appearance of the horse in Mesopotamia (Postgate, 1986: 200; Oates et al., 2008: 390; Weber, 2012: 169). It is argued among the researchers that this role was what elevated this animal to its high social and symbolic status. As a proof of it, depictions of this kind of equid pulling from vehicles can be found in royal glyptic and textiles, votive plaques and even stelae (fig. 31). The appearance of the *kúnga* in this kind of imagery and also in administrative texts implies that this animal was an elite marker and part of royal propaganda (Weber, 2012: 169).

There were breeding centers for this special hybrid that controlled its distribution, which seems restricted to royal and elite domain. One of them was Nagar. According to the texts, Ebla used to pay high amounts of money to Nagar in order to acquire exemplars of this animal (Weber, 2012: 349; 2012: 169; Oates et al., 2008: 390).

Although *kúnga* may be considered the highest esteemed type of equid in the Ancient Near East before the consolidation of the horse domestication, donkey was really close to it concerning significance, as it has been proved. Since only the wealthiest members of the elite could afford to pay for them it is likely to think that donkey was chosen instead by the less rich elites unable to do it.

FIG. 31. SOME *KÚNGA* PULLING FROM BATTLE WAGONS DEPICTED IN THE STANDARD OF UR (2600 BC) (AFTER LITTAUER & CROUWEL, 1979).

5. 2. 2. Dogs

The role of dogs in human societies is diverse all over the time and the space. The relationship between dogs and humans is complex and multi-faceted, and the use of dogs in human society goes beyond being a companion animal (Yates & Koler-Matznick, 2002: 142). The origin of dog domestication has been stated around 12.000 BP. Some believe that their first function was as sanitary workers since they used to clean the camp environs through scavenging, making them less attractive to predators (Collins, 1990: 211; Yates & Koler-Matznick, 2002: 144). Their use as hunting companion, as well as beasts of burden, is well attested in the archaeological and historical record since ancient times in both Asia and Europe. It is known that dogs have been used as food throughout the world in different cultures and periods, according to the world-wide archaeological evidence, not only in the Americas but also in several sites in Europe, including France and Britain (Yates & Koler-Matznick, 2002: 139-140). Dog parts have been also included in personal items and goods since prehistoric times, not only for ritualistic and religious purposes but also for personal adornment and trade (Yates & Koler-Matznick, 2002: 141-142). As it is widely known and studied, unlike other domestic animals, dogs have a different and special emotional value that places them closer to humans, thus becoming ritualised globally in many cultures, being even buried in human-like ceremonial burials.

One of the first documented ceremonial relationship between humans and dogs (if not the first), dating from 9600 BC, is attested in Ein Malahha (northern Israel), where a woman was found buried with a wolf or dog puppy next to her head (Davis, 1987: 145-147; Wapnish & Hesse, 1997: 166). In general, the phenomenon of dog burial is known in ancient eastern Mediterranean, although only in Egypt and Israel was practised on a large scale (Wapnish & Hesse, 1997: 166). With the exception of the dog cemetery discovered at Isin, few dog burials are attested in the ancient Near East during the third and second millennium BC. Concerning the dog burials at Isin (see section 4), it has been claimed according the osteological analysis that dogs at this site were not necessarily specially treated in life and they were probably just kicked around. Even thought with this statement it seems that the special implications of the practice of burial and even the symbolic qualities associated with dogs are forgotten. If they were just kicked out after death one may expect to find their corpses piled in a pit or a midden instead of finding each of them interred in a single burial. Furthermore, despite the fact that at first sight these dogs were not deliberately well cared for it does not necessarily mean they were not specially respected. The association with the deity and a particular sacred place are clear, and the fact that they were buried is important since burials usually involve serious and unique symbolic connotations and beliefs. What is more, since this temple was known as "the House of the Dogs" it is likely to think they probably lived in peace by their own without any disturbances and after their death they would have been properly buried, what it is in fact a special treatment by itself. It should be borne in mind that the circumstances of the dog burials in Ashkelon during the Persian period are really similar to the ones of the burials at Isin, as it has been pointed out (Hesse & Wapnish, 2008: 565-568). Despite the distance in time and space, both cases have been compared due to their likeness since dogs from Ashkelon were also regarded as pariah dogs and a pattern of interment is attested in both cemeteries, being the size of the funerary complex the only main difference. Anyway, dogs from Ashkelon have been considered revered as sacred animals. Thus, it makes sense to suggest a similar interpretation for the dog burials of Isin. Further research about the condition and details of the burials may help us with this discussion, but they are not properly provided in the bibliography.

Concerning this paper and the nature of its study we should make a distinction between adult dogs and puppies according not only to the archaeological record but also to the written sources.

Adult dogs are extremely scarce and have been recorded only in a few sites such as Nagar or Isin (previously discussed). Some of them have been found in funerary contexts displaying resemblances with other findings in Egypt and even regarding the same species, the greyhounds. It is known that species such as the *saluki* or the greyhound are one of the oldest breeds in the world, used for hunting in ancient times by the royalty and therefore widely depicted in pictorial representations from the second millennium BC in Egypt, for example (Clutton-Brock, 2001: 328-329; Hesse & Wapnish, 2008: 555-558). In this context, bearing in mind that hunting was an activity linked to the elite since only resourceful personnel could enjoy of free time to carry out this kind of activities in agricultural societies, it is likely to think that this dog species were associated to the elite, something supported by their finding in elite funerary contexts and by the iconography. However, if dogs were owned by the royal personnel and could even be used as elite markers one may expect to find them more frequently among the archaeological record, as it happens with the donkey, for example. However, and although the archaeological evidence is really limited, my suggestion is that dog scarcity within the archaeological record is due to the fact that dog did not entail the socio-economic impact that did the donkey, although I am aware of the speculative kind of this statement.

On the other hand, dogs were used in sacrificial and exorcist rites in Anatolia and sacrificed to conclude covenant rituals among the western Semites (Wapnish & Hesse, 1997: 166). It is widely known that dog was valued for its usefulness in hunting, shepherding and guarding in Hittite society, where it was used in rituals as an agent of prevention and purification. Puppies were used in rituals as the Ritual of Huwarlu to protect royal personalities from evil, as well as to prevent a bad sighting or omen. In the same way, puppies were presented as offerings in appeasement rituals in the hope of gaining the deity's help against evil and dark forces or beings or as offerings to netherworld deities, in which cases they were sacrificed (Collins, 1990: 211-214; Hesse & Wapnish, 2008: 562). It is likely to think that the symbolic value and significance of the puppy and its therefore role in rituals of different nature had an origin previous to the Hittites, in the same way that happens with both equids and ovicaprines. After all, these beliefs and ritual ceremonies associated with the puppy continues in later times even up to the Hellenistic period, where the finding of dogs and puppies within the archaeological record is much higher than in the Bronze Age, and not only in Ancient Near East but also in all the Mediterranean. The same phenomenon occurs concerning the equid and other animals, something widely attested by the written sources, as we have just seen. Thus, it is likely to think that the ritual practices and beliefs related to the puppy (and dogs in general) that appear in the Hittite sources existed also in Sumerian and Akkadian times, as they took place equally in later times.

Following this logical discussion, what the Hittite sources tell us about the role of the puppy in this kind of rituals fits in some ways the archaeological record compiled in this paper in previous sections. Unlike equids, puppies seldom appear in the archaeological record, but they do it in contexts which I firmly believe are directly related to the rituals and ceremonies narrated in the written sources. In Syria the presence of puppies is only attested in Umm el-Marra. Although this site is really singular and extraordinary, it is likely to think that similar rituals involving the use of the puppies for prevention and/or appeasement took place in it. All the puppy skeletons recorded in the third millennium BC were found closely related to graves, associated with equids and other animals. In the case of the puppies found at the burned room next to *Tomb 6* the ritual implications of their finding seems clear since they were very carefully deposited in each corner of the room and in company of a piglet, another animal that usually take part in this kind of rituals. We should not forget the fact that the room was probably deliberately burned as part of the ritual. The deposition of puppies near tombs of directly close to them may lead us to think about rituals and ceremonies of appeasement that were celebrated as part of the different funerary ceremonies. Hence, these rituals may have been done in order to do offerings for the netherworld deities. Moreover, the nature of these practices not really needed to be mutually exclusive, and the presence of puppies and other animals also as apotropaic agents seems logic. In this way, puppies might worked both as offerings and prevention of evil forces, two definitely useful roles in funerary contexts. The same scenario it is likely to have happened in Tell Madhhur, where a puppy was found inside what has been interpreted as a "chariot burial".

The symbolic uses and beliefs of puppies within the rituals and ceremonies of Ancient Near East do not end here and go far beyond. Several roles within rituals and cultic activities are also attested in the Hittite sources, uses that may be also in relation with the presented archaeological record.

Puppy, as well as donkey, was sacrificed in treaty ceremonies. An example of this could be the findings at the temple of Tel Haror, in which courtyard puppies with their neck or back broken have been buried (see section 4) (Way, 2011: 79). In addition, a belief in the dog's medical power has been widely held from ancient to modern times. It is known that dogs played a role of cultic healing and as purifying agents in Greece, Anatolia and Mesopotamia, although only in Greece were they consumed in funerary contexts (Wapnish & Hesse, 1997: 166). A puppy, being held up to the patient, was expected to cure him, a practice that might have its origin in Mesopotamia as it can be found in Babylonian magical texts. From there it could make its way to Anatolia and even later cultures such as Greece, where dogs were also used to diagnose disease, as previously stated (Collins, 1990: 214-216; Hesse & Wapnish, 2008: 562). Puppies were also used in rituals of purification for the elite personnel, where the puppy at issue was waved over the personality and worked as the bearer of the impurity (Collins, 1990: 217-218: Way, 2011: 72-73). An example of that can be found in the so-called Ritual of Tunnawi, where a piglet and even ovicaprines play also a role as purifying agents. In the Ritual of Mastigga the puppy is sacrificed and then buried in a process where the impurity is transferred to the puppy and then eliminated by the death of it (Collins, 1990: 217-218). This kind of rituals might also explain the puppy found at Tell Madhhur, for example, as a way to purify the human individual buried in the tomb. It should be borne in mind that these functions do not have to be necessarily exclusive, as I argued before.

There are several rituals of purification that involve the use of a puppy, but the severing rituals are the most common ones. Severing rituals, related to "gate rituals", involved the act of cleaving the puppy in two halves. In these rituals each half of the puppy was placed to the both sides of a gate and then the offerant walked between the gates and through the halves in a process that was supposed to extract the impurity from him or her (Collins, 1990: 218-221).

As it will be detailed below, puppies were involved in the same rituals as ovicaprines, bovids and piglets although playing different roles. It has been stated that, unlike other mentioned domestic animals whose use in this kind of rituals was more frequent (i.e., ovicaprines and bovids), the role of the dog was aimed to prevent impurity or to purify instead of being used as an offering (Collins, 1990: 225-226). In addition, it has been claimed that reasons for that lie in the fact that dog, like pig, was valueless for its unclean nature and hence an aversion for the deities as an offering sacrifice or food, something that may have reduced its roles within the cultic ceremonies, and made them the proper to be sacrificed in severing rituals over other animals (Collins, 1990: 211, 221, 225-226: Hesse & Wapnish, 2008: 562). In my personal opinion, these statements are contradictory and highly arguable according not only to the textual evidence but also to the archaeological record. First of all, the killing of a puppy in order to deliver it to a supernatural being as an offering has been attested in the written sources, as well as their sacrifice in other contexts such as the treaty ceremonies (as is stated at the beginning of this section). In this way, dogs may have been more similar concerning treatment and significance to donkeys rather than pigs, for example, and the high ideological significance of the donkey is undeniable in different ways, as it has been shown. Moreover, one would expect pigs to appear in the archaeological record as much as puppies and in similar contexts, something that does not happen in Syria nor Mesopotamia in all the Bronze Age but in Umm el-Marra, although it is true that dog and puppy findings are extremely scarce to constitute a solid basis for postulates of this kind.

Furthermore, although from the archaeological viewpoint it is difficult to assess the nature of a finding that has been considered of ritual kind, it is possible to discuss at least about the meaning of a finding as a sacrifice according to its features and the cause of death of the animals. In the case of Umm el-Marra, for example, the presence of puppy skeletons in *Shaft 1* is susceptible of being interpreted as ritual sacrifices, as discussed in section 4. What is more, the presence of a puppy in association with graves related to elite and/or royal personnel, as in the cases of Tell Madhhur or Umm el-Marra during the third millennium BC, may lead us to think about the puppy as an apotropaic and positive agent rather than something aversive to the netherworld gods, and even an offering to them. Indeed, the rituals detailed by B. J. Collins are suggestive of ceremonies taking place in a sacred space or a temple, but the articulated skeletons of puppies found in the record have been yielded from funerary contexts associated with the elite, and in some cases related to other animals of high symbolic importance such as donkeys, as previously mentioned, which supports the statements that I am currently arguing.

In addition, dog is related to healing and even with the goddess Gula, as stated before. One may not expect an unclean animal to be revered as a sacred animal associated with healing, something that does not happen with the pig, which discussion will be developed below. Indeed, from the Late Bronze Age through the Classical period dog sacrifice and burial were not uncommon in areas like Greece or Iran, where these animals could be regarded sentimentally and even imbued with ritual potency, as it has been pointed out (Hesse & Wapnish, 2008: 562). This positive ideological value seems to exist even in previous finds dated before the Bronze Age, as in the case of the burial of Ein Mallaha, for example, and it is likely to think about a positive assessment of the dog since its domestication in the Mesolithic due to its usefulness for the economy and its close relation to the human, as it has been argued. What seems clear about this discussion is that its origins lie in the existent contradiction within the archaeological record and the textual evidence since the positive role that the dog has in the Semitic culture does not fit at all with the textual evidence that provide scornful descriptions about the nature of this animal, as it has been demonstrated (Hesse & Wapnish, 2008 562).

Since the significance of the dog seems to vary throughout time and space, it is likely to think that the reason for that is the result of local and cultural peculiarities. The presence of dogs in human graves since the Neolithic and their appreciation as hunters and shepherds, something that related them to the elite, as it has been argued in this paper, does not fit the textual evidence and the framework stated, which contradicts also the later significance of this animal. Moreover, these contradictions seem to exist in all the Fertile Crescent but Egypt, where greyhounds, for example, have been always well esteemed. Since the role of dogs and puppies within the rituals of near eastern cultures seems to be multi-faced and diverse, and bearing in mind how limited is the archaeological record, it is not wise to establish such severe statements, even more if we bear in mind the contradictory nature of the evidence. It may make sense in rituals of purification where the puppy is used as a transportation of the impurity and then it is disposed of, but it is not so clear in rituals where the puppy works as an apotropaic and purifying agent related even to royal ceremonies or as offering to deities in order to ask for their support. The practice of dog burial should be also borne in mind of a special attitude towards the dog, as I discussed above even more if it appears associated with human graves. The same type of contradiction seems to exist in the case of the donkey, as it has been previously detailed, since donkey was also used in rituals of purification as the bearer of the impurity, but it was equally displayed within the funerary assemblage as a social marker.

To sum up, we can argue that a wide range of attitudes toward the dogs exists in these periods, each related to different scripts associated with the socio-ideological and political aspects of each of the cultures of these times, as it has been pointed out (from Hesse et al., 2012: 227).

5. 2. 3. Sheeps and goats

While goat was probably first domesticated in the Zagros Mountains in about 7500 BC, sheep seems to have been domesticated some time later in the more lowlands areas to the north and west (Zeder, 1997: 24). The herding of domestic ovicaprines coupled with the cultivation of cereal afforded a high level of security and predictability to the new food-producing economies of the Neolithic, resulting in new economies that entailed a restructuring of both the social organisation and the belief systems. In this context, ovicaprines continued playing a central role in the highly specialised economies of the urban societies of the fourth millennium onward (Zeder, 1997: 24). Controlling the distribution of ovicaprines had a major concern to urban administrator to the extent that the pastoral nomads became an important disruptive force in the political stability of the urban societies by the second millennium (Zeder, 1997: 24).

As well as donkeys and puppies, goats were sacrificed in covenant ceremonies (Way, 2011: 79-80), rituals of appeasement (Collins, 1990: 213-214), purifying rituals (Collins, 1990: 215, 217-218) and severing rituals (Collins, 1990: 221). Structured ovicaprines remains are susceptible of being interpreted as offerings rather than having been consumed in feasting ceremonies since the remains are not fragmented or discarded, and sometimes closely associated with human burials, as it occurs in Nippur, for example. It is interesting how both types of remains appear in some cases together in the same context, as in the case of Abu Salabikh. As it also happens with donkey and dog, it seems that these individuals played different roles but took part in the same ceremonies, ones of funerary nature in those cases. Thus, while some ovicaprines were consumed in the feasting ceremony others could have been sacrificed as offerings to underworld deities, for example.

5. 2. 4. Bovids

Domestic cattle are attested in central Anatolia, northern Syria and the Levant by the fifth millennium BC, although the process must have started earlier. In the cases of Iraq and Iran there is no evidence of domestic cattle prior to fourth millennium BC (Hesse, 1997a: 442). Concerning the plow, the first artistic evidence of it is recorded from southern Mesopotamia and dates to the fourth millennium, where osteological evidence of the use of cattle as plow has been yielded in the Levant and Anatolia (Hesse, 1997a: 443).

Cattle are very adaptable to diverse habitats, which caused isolation between regional populations, thus resulting in stock of varied appearance. Moreover, the advent of plow agriculture by the use of cattle made possible to redirect the resulting surplus labor to other activities, enhancing the potential for increased social and economic complexity (Hesse, 1997a: 442-443). Even cattle were the third most common domesticate animal found at site in the Ancient Near East, their large size and utility made them considerably more valuable (Hesse, 1997a: 443).

It is remarkable how only a few cases (standing out Umm el-Marra and Megiddo) of articulated bovid remains have been found despite their ideological value and significance towards economy and daily life, not to mention that bovids were closely related to temple economy. Bovids usually take part of the offering assemblages along with ovicaprines, thus constituting discarded bone remains in most of cases.

5. 2. 5. Pigs

According to the evidence, a difference between piglets and adult pigs might be established, as it happened with the dog. While pigs are absolute scarce within the archaeological record, some articulated skeletons of piglets have been found in contexts of ritual nature. It is known through the textual evidence that piglets were also used in rituals of purification as the Ritual of Tunnawi (Collins, 1990: 217) and in rituals of appeasement (Collins, 1990: 213-214), so it is likely to think about piglets being used as offerings in funerary contexts as it happens with other animals.

Generally, pigs, whose first trace of domestication dates to 8500 BC in the site of Hallan Cemi (Turkey), have been considered of unclean nature and therefore unsuitable for consumption in the Ancient Near East. However, theories of pig avoidance seem to have a stronger functionalist background since in some areas they were consumed as food and used in ritual ceremonies. Unlike sheep, goats and even cattle, pigs require more water and moisture to be raised, being scarce or even absent in the drier areas, and they tolerate a limited range of ecological conditions, thus the range of management strategies able to raise pigs in Near East is limited (Grigson 1995: 254; Zeder, 1998: 110-111; Ben-Shlomo et al. 2009: 141; Rowan & Golden 2009: 21). It has been stated that at sites located in areas of less than 200 mm of annual rainfall pig bones are absent. Hence, the presence or absence of pig bone remains is considered a hypothetical indicator of the level of humidity of the area in some cases, and furthermore, it reflects the rainfall patterns (Rowan & Golden 2009: 21; Gündem, 2010: 157-159). In addition, pigs are immobile and not suitable for long-distance transhumance and provide no secondary products, which make them less attractive than other livestock (Zeder, 1998: 110-111; Ben-Shlomo et al. 2009: 141). Nevertheless, the domestication of the pig offers some important advantages. The omnivorous nature of the pig makes it able to recycle waste and spoilage and convert it into a nutrient-rich food resource and its other limitations previously mentioned can be compensated by keeping it close to home and providing it with shade and wallow. And not only it is a relatively easy animal to maintain, but also it is well suited to small-scale sty management. However, it has been stated that keeping pigs close to home puts them in direct competition with human for basic food resources (Zeder, 1998: 110).

There is a reasoning argued by P. Diener and E. E. Robkin (Diener & Robkin, 1978: 493-509) that really appeals me concerning to this topic. They postulate that since pig rearing in the region was likely undertaken by small independent households, pigs did not fit well into centrally coordinated urban economies that sought to control the flow of commodities to dependent consumers. This statement may explain at least the scarcity of pig remains in the Fertile Crescent during the Bronze Age in areas of higher urbanism such as Mesopotamia or northern Syria. Furthermore, it fits the fact that pigs were a subsistence strategy particularly important in periods and places of decreased political centralisation (Hesse, 1997b: 348).

It should be borne in mind that the most likely scenario is that the cultural and ideological reasons for pig aversion may be a result of the functional disadvantages of its breeding and raising, occurring thus in areas where the pig was not incorporated to the economic system due to such disadvantages.

All societies throughout human history showed some degree of inequality, manifested specially in the distribution of material and other resources. In this context, food is an important parameter. Religion can act as a differentiating factor, which may manifest in food taboos, for example. General ideas or beliefs about health and food may origin different consumption patterns within groups, and by practising a particular religion and regulating eating practises social groups may separate themselves from the rest (O'Day et al., 2004: xii-xiii). Pig aversion may fit perfectly in this frame of discussion, as well as the negative assessments about dogs.

5. 2. 6. Birds

Articulated skeletal remains of birds have been found only in three sites: Tel Beydar and Umm el-Marra in Syria and Tel Haror in the Levant. In the case of Tel Beydar the discussion was carried out in section 3, but in this section further discussion about the vultures of Umm el-Marra (foun at *Shaft 1*) and the corvids of Tel Haror is provided. On the one hand and concerning the last ones, since not much is known about the use of *corvidae* in the ancient Near East, the individuals found at Tel Haror constitute an exceptional case. They were probably trapped with nets as they are usually portrayed as being netted in Egyptian and Mesopotamian art (Klenck, 2002: 50).

On the other hand, it has been suggested that the inclusion of vultures in the ritual deposits of Umm el-Marra may indicate they played a role as agents of dishonour, and therefore the sacrificial victims were probably vanquished enemies since this animal is usually depicted in ancient Near Eastern art feasting on the bodies of death enemies (Schwartz, 2013: 513). Following this logical discussion, these sacrifices might were made in gratitude for victory and the animal associated with them could have been victim's possessions (Schwartz, 2013: 513). Here there are several aspects that call into question such statements. First of all, the association of animals with humans in such contexts does not necessarily mean they belonged to the "victims" since animals were sacrificed in several types of offering and appeasing rituals, as it shows the whole archaeological record compiled in this paper. Secondly, further evidence is needed to confirm a warfare scenario. In such case, one may expect the site to be fortified with walls or some kind of defensive system, in addition to further archaeological indicators of violence. At last but not least, the fact that vultures were ichnographically depicted in that way does not shut out other interpretations. Discarded vulture remains have been also found in Tell Beydar, for example, and this interpretation is not likely to fit the findings of that site. Since such details are not provided in the report where G. Schwartz suggests such statements I consider them speculative rather than empirical due to the lack of evidence.

5. 2. 7. Fish

Only in Nagar (see section 3) structured bone remains of fish have been found. It has been stated that several factors suggest that the individual found in Tell Brak represents a different phenomenon than the presence of other fishes. Its presence more than 2000 km from the Gulf indicates a long-distance trade, probably carried out by land. If this kind of seabreams trade really existed, it is likely to think about it as a rare event aimed to transport also other larger specimens over such long distances, and not only yellow-fin black porgy individuals, tiny and full of spines. Furthermore, the good state of preservation of the skeleton at Tell Brak suggests a very rapid burial. Moreover, the presence of gill bones could be an indicator of the use of some kind of preservation liquid to keep the animal (Roselló Izquierdo & Morales Múñiz, 2001: 343-344).

If we bear in mind that this fish is still held in high esteem nowadays in the Persian Gulf, and that it has been found in graves generally in Mesopotamia, as it has been stated previously, it is likely to interpret it as a ritual deposit. To support this assessment, other pieces of evidence have been displayed. The first one is that in the same area where the fish skeleton was found, where copper and bronze tools and items appeared, as well as a fine Akkadian cylinder seal, all of them also considered by the researchers as ritual deposits. The second one is the small presence of other non local types of fish bones from other monumental buildings at Tell Brak, such as grunt, drum and stingray, and even evidence of a spiny fish (interpreted as a Rabbit Fish or a Porcupine Fish) depicted in an Akkadian potsherd (Roselló Izquierdo & Morales Múñiz, 2001: 344).

5. 3. Ritual and sacrifice in the frame of structured deposition of animal remains

Since the vast majority (if not all of them) of the structured deposits of animal remains have been found in ritual and/or funerary contexts, I consider convenient to develop a further discussion about ritual and religion within the framework worked out in this paper.

It is well known that people's behaviour in the past was not only directed by economic and ecological constrains but also influenced by social mechanisms which include ideology and religion in general (O'Day et al., 2004: xi). Indeed, the difference between both dimensions in ancient times was so thin that in many aspects it probably did not even exist.

While religion is considered to be a fundamental universal feature of human societies, it is often elusive or even inaccessible archaeologically. The same issue takes place concerning ritual practices, traditionally distinguished from other forms of human actions by its supposed non-utilitarian and irrational qualities (O'Day et al., 2004: xii). In this way, religious practices have been traditionally considered archaeologically identifiable since they are considered distinct from the daily practices, as it has been argued (O'Day et al., 2004: xii). Furthermore, ritual activity has been usually investigated through observations of structured or deliberate and patterned deposition of the remains, according to the statement that domestic activity is unpatterned and/or less structured (Luff, 1996: 1). All these statements are highly debatable since the circumstances surrounding a finding are many, and in the same way that a discarded bone assemblage can be of ritual kind for several reasons, structured bone remain deposits in domestic contexts can be yielded. Moreover, I shall remind how the difference between what it is sacred and what it is ordinary does not even exist in many aspects of life in ancient times. I personally agree with the statement that religion in antiquity cannot be considered an isolated compartment of social life (Pongratz-Leisten, 2012: 291). In addition, as R. Luff argues, it is important to remember that ritual need not necessarily be confined to religious phenomena since there are social rituals of secular type (Luff, 1996: 1).

Concerning animal remains, and following this logical discussion, it should be borne in mind that ethnographical, textual and archaeological evidence show us how an act of animal killing is not always easy to analyse as a domestic or a ritual one, and sometimes such difference does not even exist. In the Ancient Near East the individual slaughter of an animal was conditioned by cultural rules and precepts that provided a detailed script of how to carry out the animal killing in addition of giving a meaning to its death. Thus, the killing of an animal carried out by its owner at his house in a village was also done in the context of the cultural and religious traditions of the region at issue (Hesse et al., 2012: 218). Therefore, the ritual death of an animal does not have to happen in public or in dramatic circumstances as long as killing an animal for consumption in a rural town was sacred as well as an elaborate ceremony taking place in a temple, it was only a matter of degree, as it has been argued (Hesse et al., 2012: 217-218). In this context, the archaeological evidence of a ritual practise not always might be possibly recorded. Furthermore, activities related to the slaughtering, skinning and defleshing of an animal usually occur in sacred spaces such as temples, resulting also in a discarded and fragmented archaeological record that can be interpreted of ritual kind due to its contexts and particular features. An illustrative example of this can be found in the Early Bronze complex at Megiddo, where larger amounts of animal bone fragments (most of them ovicaprines and bovids) have been associated with the dismemberment of a carcass and other activities related to slaughtering and food production (Wapnish & Hesse, 2000: 429-449; Hesse et al., 2012: 223). In addition, we should remember that temples and sacred spaces usually worked as distributors of the resources, which means that animal remains found in domestic contexts– articulated or not–might have been previously processed in sacred spaces.

Material culture depicting and/or associated with animals may also provide clues about ideology, religious practices and the role of animals within spiritual systems (O'Day et al., 2004: xii). An example of this can be found in several "chariot burials" from the third millennium, where rein-rings depicting burden animals–that in some of these cases were the same that appeared in the burials–and zoomorphic figurines have been recorded. This also strengthens the symbolical connotations of the skeletal remains found in ritual contexts.

On the other hand, two different distinguishable categories within the phenomenon of ritual killing have been pointed out. One would consist of sacrifice as an offering to supernatural beings, which is a communicative action that also includes other liturgical and performative procedures and usually takes places in a sacred space; and the other one would be those rituals of prevention aimed to dispel evil forces, which usually takes place in open places (Pongratz-Leisten, 2012: 291). Although it is not possible to know exactly which rituals take place through the analysis of the archaeological record, it is true that ritual killing is attested in both open and closed spaces. Hence, following this logical discussion, the location of the remains may give us information about the nature of the ritual (or non-ritual) activities identified in the archaeological record.

It has been also claimed that offering ceremonies, constituting a routine for the maintenance of the cult and the system, should not be discussed under the umbrella of a universal theory of sacrifice (Pongratz-Leisten, 2012: 295). I disagree since although it is true that these ritual practices change throughout the time and the space they took place all over the Ancient Near East displaying some degree of unity despite their particularities and even sharing similar patterns, as it can be supported by both the textual and the presented archaeological evidence. Despite the diversity among the scripts of these practices, the similarity of the finds, above all concerning elite burials, witness a wider and general phenomenon of symbolic attitudes toward these animals whose roots could be considered culturally unified, as it has been argued before in this paper.

5. 4. Conclusions

It is likely to deduce according to the evidence compiled and discussed in this paper that since most of all these animal species were not only found in funerary and/or ritual contexts in a structured state of preservation but also sharing the same spaces in not only a few cases, that all these animals held symbolic and ritual connotations and had different roles in the same kind of ceremonies. The differences between the roles these animals played might be in relation with their significance towards economy and husbandry and their relation with humans. What seems clear is that there is a general phenomenon, a broad thought and attitude towards these animals that result in these ritual and cultic practices, a new attitude that seems to start consolidated in the late fourth millennium BC, although a few previous cases could be named. As E. Vila pointed out in the case of the equids, it is likely to think that this new phenomenon is related to the fact that these animals were domesticated and thus close to the human sphere, receiving special traits like been buried or sacrificed to underworld deities. Since wild animals were related to hunting, seems logic not to find structured deposition of such species, although some parts of them are used in a sacred context, as in the case of the gazelle horns.

Some questions may arise with the statement of this framework. The first of them might be why this kind of characteristic treatment is attested only in a few cases in animal species that have been domesticated previously to the late fourth millennium BC, as the cases of the sheep, the goat or the dog. One may expect these practices to occur more frequently in previous times in the cases of these animals as they are domesticated. They key problem, as it has been stated previously, is the scarcity of the archaeological record, that does not allow to develop a solid overall framework based on the evidence yielded. We may think, according to the evidence, that these practices took place gradually since the origin of animal domestication (after all, the change in the relationship between animals and humans as they are domesticated is also displayed in the iconography and art), but a first height of these practices occurs in the beginnings of the third millennium. This "new" phenomenon may continue after the Bronze Age up to Hellenistic times and even later, changing all over the time and the space although existing cultural continuity, and even maintaining the key feature: it is originally based on the relation with these animals established according to their role within the domestic economy. Therefore, these changes that took place all over the time and the space would be related to the environmental and economic particularities of each area, from which the cultural features are also born. To sum up, there is a broad religious attitude towards the main domesticated animals of human economy in the Ancient Near East, based on the closeness of these animals to the human sphere, and where the different significances associated with each animal species may be related to their role in the economy and therefore relationship with humans.

This can be supported not only by the textual evidence but also by the archaeological record. It has been pointed out how these animals take place in the same rituals at the same time but playing different roles according to their own ideological significance. In the Hittite Ritual of the Ox, for example, it is recorded how four different animals are used in the same ceremony of purification celebrated for both the king and the queen: a ram, a puppy, a sheep and a piglet (Collins, 1990: 215). In the Ritual of Anniwiyanni, a severing ritual also of purification, a goat is used as an offering to the Protective Deity while a puppy is used as a purification agent and therefore killed to complete the ritual (Collins, 1990: 221). Some other mentioned ritual as the "scape-goat" ones or the treaty ceremonies, where donkey, dogs and goats were used in the same way and with the same purposes, are additional illustrative examples.

This is also recognisable within the archaeological evidence since there are several cases of animal sharing not only the same context but also the same stratigraphy. It is not the first time that the puppy found next to two equids at Tell Madhhur is mentioned in the context of this discussion. In Abu Salabikh several structured remains of ovicaprines were found next to discarded ones and among the funerary furnishing in a grave that contained also equids. Here, different interpretations can be argued since the articulated remains of the ovicaprines may be considered offerings to the underworld deities while the equids may be interpreted as social marker and funerary furnishing, for example. Other similar cases can be recognised in Nippur, Tell Halawa and Umm el-Marra, where equids that died naturally shared space with younger ones that were deliberately killed (see section 3). I shall remind that several puppy and piglet skeletons were also found in the graves of Umm el-Marra associated with equid and even human individuals. Osteological analyses may help us with these interpretations since a well-cared for animal may differ from a younger one that has been sacrificed, but the issues of this survey have been already displayed.

6. Conclusions

Structure deposition of animal remains does not constitute a phenomenon *per se*, as it happens concerning animal ritual and burial of any kind. They are part of a general scope of attitude and significance towards these animal species, a fact related to their role in economy and subsequent impact in daily life. Thus, the different treatment and symbolic roles of these animals are a result of their relationship with humans and the particularities of the cultures at issue. As B. Hesse, P. Wapnish and J. Greer indicate regarding the Levant (Hesse et al., 2012: 217), I argue that domesticated animals were powerful constituents in the cultural landscape of these regions, never simply resources. Moreover, their deaths did not go unremarked, and complex ideologies emerged to naturalise the deaths of these animals even when they were part of a necessary process of being converted into consumable products, a framework that may explain most of the compiled findings. In addition, since there is no doubt that these animals held a special status in the ritual practices of the Ancient Near East, question may also arise regarding the ceremonial roles these animals had.

If we accept that daily life and religion cannot be separate in ancient times, not only the ritual and/or sacred aspects of the evidence should we focused on. Most of these animal species are domesticated ones and thus a reflection of the economy of these societies. Hence, changes in the treatment of these animals as well as in their appearance within the archaeological record may also reflect changes and differences in the economies of these sites, as well as particular cultural differences. Thus, further research should cover the faunal evidence from domestic contexts of these sites and periods should be examined together with the presented one, as L. Horwitz suggests for cases such as Jebel Qa'aqir and Sasa (Horwitz, 1987: 254). Only with such comparative broad method of study it could be understood how and to what extents these animals were integrated in society and economy. It should also be borne in mind that discarded faunal assemblages could have been originally deposited structured and later disassembled due to post-depositional factors, as previously argued. In the same way, they may have their origin in religious contexts- i.e., as a result of a feasting ceremony- above all in societies with a temple economy structure.

The difference of age of the animals may reflect, for example, differences in animal exploitation patterns, something also related to the ritual ceremonies and ideological significance of these animals. After all, animals kept for meat production were usually slaughtered at a young age while those kept for the production of secondary products have a high ratio of age. Thus, killing a young animal in order to obtain meat was both an "ordinary" and a sacred act, implying functional and symbolical connotations at the same time. In the same way, since the living maintain their relationship with the dead through mortuary practices, these might be a reflection of social structure and organisation, as it has been argued (Porter, 2002a: 156). A multi-disciplinary approach to animal deposition may provide us wide range information of different aspects of ancient life which may lie uncharted by applying more limited frameworks.

Moreover, as previously stated all over this essay, both literature and data concerning this framework need a deep review. On the one hand, the information provided in previous studies is partial and incomplete, and it is only possible to find a detailed analysis about faunal remains in a few cases. On the other hand, the quality of recent surveys is variable and a lack of detailed analyses concerning faunal assemblages is equally prevailing. In addition, while there have been plenty of excavations in sites located in Syria and Mesopotamia and dating to the III Millennium BC and only a few cases of study in the Levant, we find the opposite scenario in the following millennium. Thus, a review of former studies, a better and more detailed analysis of faunal remains in current surveys and a wider and more diverse fieldwork labor are necessary for a better understanding not only of this phenomenon but also of any topic concerning zooarchaeology and economy in ancient times.

Bibliography

Baadsgaard, A., Monge, J. & Zettler, R. L. (2012): "Bludgeoned, burned, and beautified: reevaluating mortuary practices in the Royal Cemetery of Ur". In Porter, A. M. & Schwartz, G. M. (eds.), *Sacred killing: the archaeology of sacrifice in the Ancient Near East*. Winona Lake, Indiana: Eisenbrauns.

Ben-Shlomo, D., Hill, A. C. & Garfinkel, Y. (2009): "Feasting between the Revolutions: Evidence from Chalcolithic Tel Tsaf, Israel". *Journal of Mediterranean Archaeology* 222, 129-150.

Bökönyi, S. (1977): "The animal remains from four sites in the Kermanshah Valley, Iran". In Bökönyi, S (ed.), *Asiab, Sarab, Dehsavar and Siahbid: the faunal evolution, environmental changes and development of animal husbandry, VIII-III millennia B.C.* Oxford: British Archaeological Reports.

Campbell, E. F. (2002): *Shechem III: the stratigraphy and architecture of Shechem/Tell Balâtah. Vol. 1: Text*. Boston: American Schools of Oriental Research.

Collins, B. J. (1990): "The puppy in the Hittite ritual". *Journal of Cuneiform Studies* 42/2, 221-226.

Clutton-Brock, J. (1986): "Osteology of the equids from Sumer". In Meadow, R. H. & Uerpmann, H. P. (eds.), *Equids in the Ancient World*. Wiesbaden: Reichert.

Clutton-Brock, J. (2001): "Ritual burials of a dog and six domestic donkeys". In Oates, D., Oates. J & MCDonald, H (eds.), *Excavations at Tell Brak Vol. 2: Nagar in the third millennium BC*: 327-338. London: British School of Archaeology in Iraq.

Clutton-Brock, J. & Burleigh, R. (1978): "The animal remains from Abu Salabikh: preliminary report". *Iraq* 40/2, 89-100.

Croft, P. (2004): "The osteological remains (mammalian and avian)". In Ussishkin, D. (ed.), *The renewed archaeological excavations at Lachisch (1973-1994), Vol. I-V*. Tel Aviv: Emery and Claire Yass publications in archaeology.

Davis, S. J. M. (1987): *The Archaeology of Animals*. New Haven & London: Yale University Press.

Diener, P. & Robkin, E. E. (1978): Ecology and evolution and the search for cultural origins: the question of Islamic pig prohibition. *Current Anthropology* 19, 493-540.

Doument-Serhal, C. (2013): *Sidon: 15 years of excavations*. Beirut: Lebanese British Friends of the National Museum.

Gibson, McG. (1972): *The City and Area of Kish*. Miami: Field Research Projects.

Gibson, M. (1981): "Differential distribution of Faunal Material at Razuk". In Gibson, M (ed.), *Uch Tepe II*. Chicago: University of Chicago, Oriental Institute.

Gibson, M., Sanders, M. C., & Mortensen, N. (1981): "Tell Razuk: stratigraphy, architecture, finds". In Gibson, M. (ed.), *Uch Tepe I*. Chicago: University of Chicago, Oriental Institute.

Grigson, C. (1995): "Plough and Pasture in the Early Economy of the Southern Levant". In Levy, T. E. (ed.), *Archaeology of Society in the Holy Land*. Leicester: Leicester University Press.

Gündem, Y. (2010):"Animal based subsistence economy of Emar during the Bronze Age". In Finkbeiner, U. & Sakal, F. (eds.), *Subartu, vol. XXV: Emar after the closure of the Tabqa Dam: the Syrian-German excavations 1996-2002*. Turnhout: Brepols.

Guy, P. L. O. (1938): *Megiddo tombs*. Chicago: University of Chicago Press.

Hesse, B. (1997a): "Cattle and oxen". In: Meyers, E. M. (ed.): *The Oxford Encyclopedia of Archaeology in the Near East, Vol. 1*. Oxford: Oxford University Press.

Hesse, B. (1997b): "Pigs". In: Meyers, E. M. (ed.): *The Oxford Encyclopedia of Archaeology in the Near East, Vol. 4*. Oxford: Oxford University Press.

Hesse, B. & Wapnish, P. (2008): "The Ashkelon dog burials: data and interpretations". In: Stager, L. E., Schloen, J. D. & Master, D. M. (eds.): *Ashkelon 1: introduction and overview (1985-2006)*. Indiana: Eisenbrauns.

Hesse, B., Wapnish, P. & Greer, J. (2012): "Scripts of Animal Sacrifice in Levantine Culture-History". In Porter, A. & Schwartz, G. M. (eds.), *Sacred Killing: The Archaeology of Sacrifice in the Ancient Near East*. Winona Lake: Eisenbrauns.

Hilzheimer, M. (1941): *Animal remains from Tell Asmar*. Chicago: The University of Chicago Press.

Horwitz, L. K. (1987): "Animal offerings from two Middle Bronze Age tombs". *Israel Exploration Journal* 37/4, 251-255.

Katz, J. C. (2000): *The Archaeology of Cult in Middle Bronze Age Canaan: The Sacred Area at Tel Haror*. PhD dissertation, University of Pennsylvania.

Killick, R & Roaf, M. (1979): "Excavations at Tell Madhur". *Sumer* 35/1-2, 534-542.

Klenck, D. J. (2002): *The Canaanite Cultic Milieu: the zooarchaeological evidence from Tel Haror, Israel*. Oxford: BAR International Series.

Leger, A. J. (1988): "Floral and faunal remains". In Seger, D. S. & Lance, H. D. (eds.), *Gezer V: the Field I caves*. Jerusalem: Nelson Glueck School of Biblical Archaeology.

Leger, A. J. & Zeder, M. (1988): "Faunal analysis". In Seger, D. S. & Lance, H. D. (eds.), *Gezer V: the Field I caves*. Jerusalem: Nelson Glueck School of Biblical Archaeology.

Lev-Tov, J. (2006): "The faunal remains: animal economy in the Iron Age I". In: Meehl, M. W., Dothan, T. & Gitin, S. (eds): *Tel Miqne-Ekron excavations 1995-1996: Field INE east slope: Iron Age I (Early Philistine Period)*. Jerusalem: W.F. Albright Institute of Archaeological research and Institute of Archaeology, Hebrew University of Jerusalem.

Littauer, M. A. & Crouwel, J. H. (1979): *Wheeled vehicles and ridden animals in the Ancient Near East*. Leiden: E. J. Brill.

Luff, R. (1996): "The 'bare bones' of identifying ritual behaviour in the archaeological record". In: Anderson, S. & Boyle, K. (eds.): *Ritual treatment of human and animal remains: proceedings of the first meeting of the Osteoarchaeological research Group*. Oxford: Oxbow.

Mackay, E. J. H. & Murray, M. A, (1952): *Ancient Gaza V*. London: British School of Archaeology in Egypt.

Mahern, E. F. (2012): "Mortuary faunal remains". In: Ben-Shlomo, D. (ed.): *The Azor cemetery: Moshe Dothan's excavations, 1958 and 1960*. Jerusalem: Israel Antiquities Authority.

McMahon, A. (2006): *Nippur V, the Early Dynastic to Akkadian transition: the Area WF sounding at Nippur*. Chicago: Oriental Institute of the University of Chicago.

Milevski, I (2011): *Early Bronze Age goods exchange in the Southern Levant: a Marxist perspective*. London: Equinox.

O'Day, S. J., Van Neer, W. & Ervynck. A. (eds.) (2004): *Behaviour behind bones: the zooarchaeology of ritual, religion, status and identity*. Oxford: Oxbow.

Oates, J., Molleson, T. & Soltysiak, A. (2008): "Equids and an acrobat: closure rituals at Tell Brak". *Antiquity* 82, 390-400.

Philip, G (1995): "Warrior burials in the Ancient Near-Eastern Bronze Age: the evidence from Mesopotamia, Western Iran and Syria-Palestine. In Campbell, S & Green, A. (eds.), *The Archaeology of Death in the Ancient Near East*. Oxford: Oxbow books.

Pongratz-Leisten, B. (2012): "Sacrifice in the Ancient Near East: offering and ritual killing". In Porter, A. M. & Schwartz, G. M. (eds.), *Sacred killing: the archaeology of sacrifice in the Ancient Near East*. Winona Lake: Eisenbrauns.

Porter, A. (2002a): "Communities in Conflict: death and the conquest for social order in the Euphrates River Valley". *Near Eastern Archaeology* 65:3, 156-173.

Porter, A. (2002b): "The dynamics of death: ancestors, pastoralism, and the origins of the third millennium city in Syria". *Bulletin of the American School of Oriental Research* 325, 1-36.

Postgate, J. N. (1986): "Equids in Sumer, Again". In Meadow, R. H. & UEerpmann, H. P. (eds.), *Equids in the Ancient World*. Wiesbaden: Reichert.

Roselló Izquiero, E. & Morales Ruiz, A. (2001): "Fish offerings from Tell Brak? Comments on an articulated specimen found in the 1990 season". In Oates, D., Oates. J & McDonald, H (eds.), *Excavations at Tell Brak Vol. 2: Nagar in the third millennium BC*: 339-345. London: British School of Archaeology in Iraq.

Rowan, Y. M. & Golden, J. (2009): "The Chalcolithic Period of the Southern Levant: A Synthetic Review". *Journal of World Prehistory* 22, 1-92.

Schwartz, G. M. (2013): "Memory and its Demolition: Ancestors, Animals and Sacrifice at Umm el-Marra, Syria". *Cambridge Archaeological Journal*, 23, 495-522.

Van Neer, W. (2000): "Faunal remains from an Akkadian grave in Tell Beydar". In Van Lerberghe, K. & Voet, G. (eds.), *Subartu 6, Tell Beydar: environmental and technical studies*. Brepols: Turnhout.

Van Neer, W. & De Cupere, B. (2000): "Faunal remains from Tell Beydar". In Van Lerberghe, K. & Voet, G. (eds.), *Subartu 6, Tell Beydar: environmental and technical studies*. Brepols: Turnhout.

Vila, E. (2006): "Data on Equids from late fourth and third millennium sites in Northern Syria". In Mashkour, M. (ed.), *Equids in time and space: papers in honour of Véra Eisenmann: proceedings of the 9th Conference of the International Council of Archaeozoology, Durham, August 2002*. Oxford: Oxbow books.

Von der Driesch, A. & Amberger, G. (1981): "Ein altababylonisches Eselkelett vom Tell Ababra/Iraq". *Bonner zoologische Beiträge* 32/1-2, 67-74.

Wapnish, P. (1997): "Middle Bronze Age burials at Tell Jemmeh and the re-examination of a purportedly 'Hyksos' practice". In: Oren, E. D. (ed.): *Hyksos: new historical and archaeological perspectives*. Philadelphia: University Museum.

Wapnish, P. & Hesse, B. (1997): "Dogs". In Meyers, E. M. (ed.), *The Oxford Encyclopedia of Archaeology in the Near East, Vol. 2*. Oxford: Oxford University Press.

Wapnish, P. & Hesse, B. (2000): "Mammal remains from the Early Bronze sacred compound". In: Finkelstein, I., Ussishkin, D. & Halpern, B. (eds.): *Megiddo III: the 1992-1996 seasons*. Tel Aviv: Institute of Archaeology, University of Tel Aviv.

Way, K. C. (2011): *Donkeys in the Biblical World: ceremony and symbol*. Wynona Lake, Ind: Eisenbrauns.

Way, K. C. (2010): "Assessing Sacred Asses: Bronze Age Donkey Burials in the Near East". *Levant* 42, 210-225.

Weber, J. A. (2001): "A preliminary assessment of Akkadian and Post-Akkadian animal exploitation at Tell Brak". In Oates, D., Oates. J & McDonald, H (eds.), *Excavations at Tell Brak Vol. 2: Nagar in the third millennium BC*: 345-350. London: British School of Archaeology in Iraq.

Weber, J. A. (2008): "Elite equids: redefining equid burials of the mid- to late 3rd millennium BC from Umm el-Marra, Syria". In Vila, E., Gourichon, L. Choyke, A. & Buitenhuis, H. (eds.), *Archaeozoology of the Near East VIII: Proceedings of the eighth international Symposium on the Archaeozoology of southwestern Asia and adjacent areas, Tome II. Actes du 8e colloque international de l'A.S.W.A. tenu à Lyon du 28 juin au 1er juillet 2006*. Paris.

Weber, J. A. (2012): "Restoring Order: Death, Display, and Authority". In Porter, A. & Schwartz, G. M. (eds.), *Sacred Killing: The Archaeology of Sacrifice in the Ancient Near East*. Winona Lake: Eisenbrauns.

Wooley, C. L. (1934): *The Royal Graves of Ur, Ur Excavations, Volume 2*. London: British Museum.

Yates, B. C. & Koler-Matznick, J. (2002): "The Evidentiary Dog: A Review of Anthrozoological Cases and Archaeological Studies". In Snyder, L. M. & Moore, E. A. (eds.), *Dogs and people in social, working, economic of symbolic interaction*. Oxford: Oxbow books.

Zarins, J (1986): "Equids associated with human burials in third millennium BC. Mesopotamia: two complimentary facets". In Meadow, R. H. & Uerpmann, H. P. (eds.), *Equids in the Ancient World*. Wiesbaden: Reichert.

Zeder, M. A. (1997): "Sheep and goats". In: Meyers, E. M. (ed.): *The Oxford Encyclopedia of Archaeology in the Near East, Vol. 5*. Oxford: Oxford University Press.

Appendix A.
Number of articulated animal individuals recorded at each site classified by specie, region and period.

In this appendix the total number of articulated animal skeletons found in the sites displayed in this survey is compiled. A symbol of (-) in the box means that no articulated skeletons of that specie have been found. On the other hand, a symbol of (*) in the box means that articulated skeletal remains of the specie at issue have been found but either it has not been possible to count them due to their state of preservation or there is not enough information about them in the reports.

Appendix A. A. Number of articulated animal individuals recorded at each site in Syria in the third millennium BC.

Site	Equids	Bovids	Ovicaprines	Dogs	Pigs	Birds	Fish
Tell Beydar	-	-	-	-	-	2	-
Umm el-Marra	25	1	-	10	1	-	-
Tel Halawa	3	-	2	-	-	-	-
Tell Banat	*	-	-	-	-	-	-
Abu Hamad	3	-	-	-	-	-	-
Tall Bi'a	1	-	-	-	-	-	-
Tell Brak	6	-	-	1	-	-	1

Appendix A. B. Number of articulated animal individuals recorded at each site in Mesopotamia/Iraq in the third millennium BC.

Site	Equids	Bovids	Ovicaprines	Dogs	Other
al-'Usiyah	4	-	-	-	-
Tell Madhhur	6	-	-	1	-
Uch Tepe	2	-	-	-	-
Tell Abu Qasim	*	-	-	-	-
Kish	*	*	-	-	-
Abu Salabikh	6	-	*	-	-
Nippur	1	-	3	-	-
Lagash	1	-	-	-	-
Ur	-	10	-	-	-

Appendix A. C. Number of articulated animal individuals recorded at each site in Mesopotamia/Iraq in the second millennium BC.

Site	Equids	Bovids	Ovicaprines	Dogs	Other
Tell Ababra	*	-	-	-	-
Isin	-	-	-	33	-

Appendix A. D. Number of articulated animal individuals recorded at each site in the Levant in the second millennium BC.

Site	Equids	Bovids	Ovicaprines	Dogs	Pigs	Birds
Azor	*	-	-	-	-	-
Sasa	-	-	-	-	-	-
Tell 'Akko	1	-	-	-	-	-
Megiddo	-	1	-	-	-	-
Sidon	-	-	1	-	-	-
Shechem	1	-	1	-	-	-
Jericho	15	-	10	-	-	-
Gezer	1	1	-	-	-	-
Tell Beth-Shemesh	1	-	-	-	-	-
Jebel Qa'aqir	-	-	20	-	-	-
Tell el-'Ajjul	2	-	-	-	-	-
Tell Jemmeh	1	-	-	-	-	-
Tel Haror	2	-	-	2	-	2

Appendix B.
Identification of equid species classified by site and period.

Equids species identified from the sites compiled in this essay are detailed below. A symbol of (-) in the box means that no articulated equid skeletons have been found. On the other hand, a symbol of (*) in the box means that articulated skeletal remains of equids have been found but it has not been possible to know the minimal number of individuals.

Appendix B. A. Specie identification of equid individuals from sites dated to the third millennium BC.

Site	Donkey	Onager	Hybrid (*kúnga*)	Unidentified
Syria				
Umm el-Marra	-	-	25	-
Tell Brak	5	-	1	-
Tall Bi'a	1	-	-	-
Abu Hamad	3	-	-	-
Tell Banat	*	*	*	-
Tell Halawa	3	-	-	-
Mesopotamia				
Al-'Usiyah	-	-	-	1
Tell Madhhur	2	-	-	2
Uch Tepe	2	-	-	-
Kish	4	-	-	*
Abu Salabikh	-	-	1	5
Nippur	-	-	-	1
Lagash	-	1	-	-

Appendinx B. B. Specie identification of equid individuals from sites dated to the second millennium BC.

Site	Donkey	Onager	Hybrid	Unidentified
Syria				
Umm el-Marra	-	-	-	6
Mesopotamia				
Tell Ababra	1	-	-	-
Levant				
Azor	-	-	-	*
Tell 'Akko	1	-	-	-
Shechem	-	-	-	1
Jericho	3	-	-	12
Gezer	1	-	-	-
Tell Beth-Shemesh	1	-	-	-
Tell el-'Ajjul	1	-	-	*
Tel Haror	1	-	-	-